D0923287

# Soldier, Soldier
# and other plays

*by the same author*

★

THE WATERS OF BABYLON

LIVE LIKE PIGS

SERJEANT MUSGRAVE'S DANCE

THE HAPPY HAVEN

THE BUSINESS OF GOOD GOVERNMENT

THE WORKHOUSE DONKEY

IRONHAND
(adapted from Goethe's *Goetz von Berlichingen*)

LEFT-HANDED LIBERTY

ARMSTRONG'S LAST GOODNIGHT

# Soldier, Soldier

## AND OTHER PLAYS

### by
### John Arden

LONDON
METHUEN & CO LTD
11 NEW FETTER LANE EC4

*First published 1967*
© *1967 by John Arden*
*All rights reserved*

*Printed in Great Britain by*
*W. & J. Mackay & Co Ltd*
*Fair Row, Chatham, Kent*

## A DEDICATION:

To
Mary Mary quite contrary
She played her whistle like a wild weird fairy
Then found the fish-shop shuttered and locked
She kicked John Balfour's haycock till it rocked
Yet all she brought down out of it was hay
None the less she swore she'd caper while she may
She took possession of an old old King of France
By God may she long continue to lead us all in such a dance!

# Contents

# Contents

# Preface

Two television plays, one one-act stage play, and an unclassifiable eccentric – all four in some way unsatisfactory: but it is pleasant to have them published, because they are all experiments of one sort or another, and, after all, the essence of an experiment is that it must imply a strong chance of failure.

In *Soldier, Soldier* the experiment was to try to see if verse was a possibility on the small screen. I am now not at all sure that it is much of a possibility on the large stage (though I still go on using it, at intervals, because I am always finding myself unable to say what I want without it): and I do not believe that *Soldier, Soldier* justified itself as a verse play. Such success as it had was due to its comic or satiric qualities, to its use of music, to the talents of the cast, and to the raucous vitality of Stuart Burge's production. I had been able to work very closely with Mr Burge before and during rehearsals (a circumstance made possible by his accommodating disposition – *not*, I should emphasize, by any policy of the BBC; more of that later), and he helped me to eliminate the potential embarrassments of this sort of writing. Because even in the theatre verse can be embarrassing, and how much more so on television with its increased intimacy. This intimacy is due to the smallness of the TV audience. It is not, in my opinion, correct to think of it as a *mass* medium. It addresses itself, on average, to two or three people only, in their own homes, at a range of two or three yards. It is not usual to speak in verse under such circumstances, except for amorous purposes or during a regular poetry-reading. But a regular poetry-reading should involve some interplay between reader and hearer, and this the television cannot supply. When the poetry is of a bardic or rhetorical style, such interplay may not be necessary: but *Soldier, Soldier* is a low-life comedy and does not come into this category. In so far as the verse of the play is colloquial and humorous, it is satisfactory: but where I allowed myself to fall into a more lyrical mood, it failed to work.

*Wet Fish* was an attempt to present on the screen a fictional version of one of my own experiences during the two years I spent as an inefficient assistant in an architect's office. I wrote the play deliberately in a flat and naturalistic manner – having learnt something from *Soldier, Soldier* – in the hope that it would prove possible to use the documentary potential of the television medium to give greater vividness to my main theme – which is, of course, the physical progress of an ill-starred building contract. I had some idea that a use of architect's plans and models, combined with realistic shots of the building work itself, would assist and, in some sequences, replace the dialogue. I did not bother to put all this into my stage directions, because I was under the impression that the play was to be directed by Mr Burge, and I was confident that I could explain it all to him more convincingly than I could write it down. Things did not turn out quite like this. Mr Burge was unable to direct *Wet Fish* and I then found myself faced with the intolerable situation that our television networks have prepared for authors who get above themselves. Another director was appointed who showed no desire to meet me. There is a policy over television contracts which apparently is founded upon the Median and Persian principle of altering not. The network authorities call it 'protecting themselves against outside interference': and it means, in practice, that they will not permit a writer to have it written in his contract that he should approve choice of director and cast. I do not know why he should not – in my experience in the theatre I have usually had this right of approval granted without question.

There is, anyway, an easy let-out for a management faced

with a difficult author. It comes in a clause which states that this approval is not to be 'unreasonably withheld'. Of course, if one were to take a quarrel of this nature into the courts, one would find that the professional experience of a producer (unless he was an obvious drunk or something) would count for much more than that of an author – if only because he must almost inevitably have produced more plays than the author could have had time to write. In any case an author's objections to directors or actors are usually 'unreasonable' hunches – which may none the less be correct.

Be that as it may, there is a certain contractual protection provided for the writer in the theatre which is unobtainable in television: and when *Wet Fish* was presented I felt the lack of it. My notions of the style of presentation were not consulted (indeed, I myself was not consulted, nor invited to rehearsals) and the fact that I had written at least two parts for specific actors was ignored. So the particular experiment I wanted to try with this play was left unattempted. It worked quite well as a straight situation comedy. I hope it will also read quite well in that capacity, for that is all it has ever been.

*When is a Door not a Door?* This little piece was specially written for a class of student actors and the experiment here was to provide parts in a play of specified length for a specified list of young men and women. I don't think the cast were very fond of the play. It did seem to offer all of them a little and none of them very much – but I was asked not to write star parts for any of them, as it was supposed to be a sort of diploma piece, in which they would all have an equal chance. This was a very artificial situation and in the event most of their talents were reduced to the speed with which they could scamper round the stage. I enjoyed writing it, however, as a purely technical exercise, and I enjoyed seeing them do it – I have never been a fanatical upholder of the idea that the inspired writer should not lower himself to commissioned work even when the conditions are so stringent as to apparently cramp his style. Mr Cartland, who directed the students in this play, did, however, succeed in discovering a mode for the production which went far to outweigh the rather stilted manner of the writing – he deliberately ignored my own requests for a 'completely realistic' style and instead developed a kind of *commedia dell' arte* fantasy which was really far more suited to the work as it stood. It is not in truth a realistic play – nor is it entirely a farce, although it has certain tendencies in that direction. I had thought I had written a contribution to naturalist theatre: Mr Cartland disagreed: and on seeing his presentation of the piece I was persuaded he was right.

With *Friday's Hiding* the experiment was to write a play for a mime. I have always had some facility at constructing dialogue which was of little use here. But thanks to Miss D'Arcy I did contrive a form with which – in the end – we were able to feel a moderate satisfaction. But as this form was one to which we were both unaccustomed, we did not feel that we should be able to test the value of our ideas until we had spent some time with the actors at rehearsal. Unfortunately the rehearsals were held a long way away from us at short notice and we never got to them: so from our point of view the experiment was almost useless. Nor did we see the finished production.

I seem to have been harping quite a lot upon the bad feelings produced in the writer by his not being encouraged to do what many will consider the job of the director. But is it the job of the director? Only, I would hazard, if the play is written in a style which is completely traditional and which requires no readjustment on the part of the actors of their normal methods of work. The only play in this book which comes under that heading is *When is a Door not a Door?* When a piece involves anything new in terms of style of writing, or staging, only the author knows exactly what is wanted, and at times not even the author. The director must learn it from him, and it is often impossible for either of them to find the exact solution to various problems until rehearsals have already commenced. Therefore it is essential that an author should always be asked to rehearsals and to early discussions with the director – even if the play appears a pretty simple one on the surface. It may not be as simple as all that. Usually I have found theatrical managements understand this and prove accommodating. Television is another matter. If the television companies do not make some adjustments in their policy towards authors, *Soldier, Soldier* and *Wet Fish* will be the only television plays I shall ever have written. The policy, I hasten to add, is an *office* policy rather than a directors' policy (though my experience with *Wet Fish* suggests that there are directors who approve it). I regard it as indefensible and a possible reason why so many television plays are not quite as good as they should have been. It is all a great pity, because television audiences include thousands of people who would never see one's work in the theatre, and television technique is attractive and stimulating to me.

JOHN ARDEN, 1966

# Soldier, Soldier

*A Comic Song for Television*

1957

*Soldier, Soldier* was first presented by BBC Television on 16 February 1960 with the following cast:

| | |
|---|---|
| A SOLDIER | Andrew Keir |
| LANDLORD | Stuart Saunders |
| JOE PARKER | Maurice Denham |
| JIM | Frank Atkinson |
| MARY | Margaretta D'Arcy |
| CHARLIE SCUFFHAM | Frank Finlay |
| MRS SCUFFHAM | Anna Wing |
| MRS PARKER | Edna Petrie |
| PUB PIANIST ⎫<br>SALVATIONIST ⎭ | John Wilding |
| NEWSPAPER BOY | Leonard Davey |

IN THE PUB ⎧ John Ringrose    Tom Payne
            Roy Denton    Gladys Dawson
            Charles Ross    Christopher May
          ⎩ Alex Foster

Directed by Stuart Burge

*Street.*
*Music: 'Soldier, Soldier' played very vigorous on drums and fifes.*
*A pair of feet in well-bulled army boots and tartan trews striding along a stone-sett street.*
*Sound of railway trains, etc.*
*A pub at the corner, to which the owner of the feet (the* SOLDIER*) is rapidly making his way, his back to the camera.*
*He goes with a fine flash swagger, twirling his little cane. It is dusk.*


*Inside the pub.*
*Close-up of an engraved-glass panel at the top of a door reading 'Railway Arms': 'Public Bar'. The door swings open and crashes shut.*
*The screen is filled with the back view of the* SOLDIER *as he strides across the floor to the bar counter.*
*The* LANDLORD *is busy polishing his counter and glasses.*
*The* SOLDIER *stops, facing the* LANDLORD*, who is too occupied to serve him for the moment.*
*The music stops, and we hear the various strands of conversation from the as yet invisible customers.*


FIRST VOICE. Aye now, but you look at it this road: a centre-half's a centre-half, I mean choose what . . .

SECOND VOICE. You can't call him a full-back . . .

THIRD VOICE. I tell you he was a sick man at the time. Bound to distort his judgement.

FOURTH VOICE. Never lifted his head, never lifted his head again . . . Take it which way you like.

SOLDIER (*suddenly lifts his chin and bellows*). Git on parade! (*All the talking stops.*)
One-two-three, two-two three, Three!

(*He beats both fists on the bar, and shouts all in a gabble*):

Who comes here?
A Fusilier,
What does he want?
He wants his beer.
Where's his money?
Here's his money.

(*He tosses a pocketful of miscellaneous money on to the bar, and exhorts the* LANDLORD.)
Smarten it up, mucker, there's a soldier wants his drink.

*We now see the rest of the room and its occupants. It is a dreary little working-class tavern, with only a few customers.*
*These are all men, mostly elderly and nondescript, sitting or standing in small gloomy groups.*
*One man,* JOE PARKER, *is at a table alone. He is about fifty, short, bald and seedy, with an inquisitive twitching nose and a Hitler moustache. His suit has a buttoned-up air of down-at-heel respectability, and he wears a collar and tie. His hat is an old black Homburg.*

LANDLORD (*sour*). There's a soldier's *had* his drink, if you ask me . . . All right, all right, chum, what'll it be?
SOLDIER. Stingo.
LANDLORD. Stingo.
SOLDIER. Stingo.
LANDLORD. Pint?
SOLDIER. Pint.
LANDLORD. Pint you are then . . . Steady, mucker, easy steady with it now.

*The* SOLDIER *is lifting the glass high up in front of him with both hands.*
*The* LANDLORD *watches this operation apprehensively. The* SOLDIER *slowly carries it to its zenith, then tilts it suddenly and deftly pours the contents into his mouth.*

SOLDIER.

> Easy steady up she goes . . .
> Up and over
> The walls of Dover:
> Here we go down into Folkestone town.

(*The glass is drained in one operation. He sets it down and takes a great breath. There is some mild applause. The* SOLDIER *turns round, leans back against the bar, and surveys the room. For the first time we see his face. He is a big tall man of thirty-five, with black hair and fierce hatchet features. He is dressed very smartly in tartan trews, blue walking-out tunic and a blue Balmoral bonnet. His accent is hard lowland Scots.*)

> This is no flaming Folkestone, this town.
> Where stands the man'll
> Tell me the name of *this* town?

LANDLORD. Not know the name of it, mucker?

SOLDIER.

> Not know the name of it.
> How should I know the name?
> All that I did was get out of a train.
> 'What station's this one?' I asked him,
> I asked him on the platform . . .
> Now where I want to get to . . .
> *I* want to get to Aldershot.

LANDLORD. We're over two hundred miles from Aldershot.

SOLDIER.

> But I only got off for a cup of tea;
> I only got off for a sandwich.
> Two minutes only to get a cup of . . .
> I've gone and missed the train.
> How can I get to Aldershot tonight?

LANDLORD. Oh, you'll not be able to now, while tomorrow morning. You'll be able to stop here, mate. You ought to have looked sharp, you ought. They never wait long for you at

this station, y'know. It's not even always what they call a
scheduled stop.

SOLDIER.

    Stay here? Stay where?

    Did I not say a sandwich!

    Never a man alive tonight

    To sell me one sandwich.

    What sort of toss-eyed town . . .

(*He suddenly beats his fists again on the bar.*)

    Stingo!

*The* LANDLORD *refills his glass, and he drinks it moodily,
slumped over the bar.*
*The general conversation now resumes.*

FIRST VOICE. How many seasons has he played, you tell me
that?

SECOND VOICE. That's nowt but evading the point; he's done
and he's done. Politics is politics.

THIRD VOICE. And that's all there is to it.

FIRST VOICE. How many seasons?

FOURTH VOICE. Well, you take Churchill now, I mean take
him and look at him . . .

PARKER *has not taken his eyes off the* SOLDIER.

PARKER. There's a train about ten o'clock in t'morning,
Serjeant: take you via London.

SOLDIER (*who is a private*).

    Serjeant he calls me. Serjeant.

    So hear him he gives praise

    To the glory where it's due.

    The Lord preserve ye for that word, man,

    Prosperity be yours

    And uncounted Posterity.

(*He swings round at the* LANDLORD.)

Do *you* hold any sandwich?

One sandwich in this house?

LANDLORD (*shaking his head*). Potato crisps. Pickled gherkin. Popcorn.

SOLDIER (*disgusted*).

Nor never one sandwich

Ham, egg, nor cheese,

For a solitary travelling man.

PARKER (*suddenly*). Caledonian Fusiliers.

SOLDIER (*sharply*). What?

PARKER. Aye? Am I right? I'll tell you: I thought I knew the badge.

SOLDIER (*fiercely contemptuous*).

Ye thought ye knew the badge.

Ye thought ye knew the . . .

Hey, mucker, hey, will I tell ye about this badge!

(*He grips* PARKER *by the lapel, and, taking off his bonnet, thrusts the badge into his eyes.*)

Caledonian Fusiliers.

A DRINKER (*to another*). Warn't that the regiment that Charlie Scuffham's lad joined up in?

SECOND DRINKER. Nay, I don't know . . .

FIRST DRINKER. I reckon it was. Eh, what a cockeyed business that affair, warn't it . . .

SOLDIER.

Observe there's words set down, it's a motto,

Can ye read it, hey, can ye read?

PARKER (*flurried*). Wait, steady on, Serjeant . . .

SOLDIER (*relentless*). There's important words are here set down . . .

PARKER (*nervously appeasing*).

Aye, I know: I can see them.

Wrote – like – in Scotch, isn't it, Serjeant?

Very interesting.

Fa fa, what is it, fo fa . . .

SOLDIER (*grandly*).
> 'Foul may fa' oor foes thegither.'
> Or in plain Saxon, mucker,
> 'Here's two fists of clouds of thunder:
> Stand out of their road
> Because there's lightnings dance between them!'

(*He has replaced his bonnet on his head, and now thrusts his clenched fists under* PARKER'S *nose.*)

> Two fists of a Fusilier:
> Two fists of the only regiment
> Has never ever even once been beat.
> Except that time by the Frenchman;
> But then there was a war.

LANDLORD. What about the other times?

SOLDIER (*whirling round*). What other times?

LANDLORD.
> When there warn't no war.
> When there was nowt but peaceful shepherds
> To never ever beat you.

*A voice down the room among laughter.*

A VOICE. Tell us about them shepherds, mate, eh.

SOLDIER.
> Aye, man, I'll tell ye.
> But first I will finish the drink:
> Get good beer beneath your middle
> Ye'll fight like a horse
> And sing like a fiddle.

*While the* SOLDIER *finishes his drink, one* DRINKER *leans against the bar at the far end of it and watches him humorously.*

DRINKER (*to no one in particular*).
> All them peaceable shepherds, he says.
> Eh, the Army, *I* don't know . . .

(*The* DRINKER *laughs and beckons the* LANDLORD.)

(*Confidentially*). What's up with Nosey Parker tonight? It's not as a general rule he wants to talk to soldiers.

LANDLORD (*also confidentially*). Unless about his principles. We've not heard overmuch about them principles tonight, have we?

DRINKER. I wonder why not.

LANDLORD (*significantly*). Caledonian Fusiliers.

DRINKER. Eh?

LANDLORD. It's not over often you see Scotchmen in this town, and specially Fusiliers.

DRINKER. What are you talking about?

LANDLORD. Old Charlie Scuffham, the window-cleaner. What was the name of that young lad of his?

DRINKER. Oh, you mean Tommy Scuffham?

LANDLORD. Aye, Tommy. *You* know.

DRINKER (*apparently enlightened*). Oh. Oh, aye.

LANDLORD (*suddenly looking up, alarmed*). Watch out, mate, watch out . . .

*The* SOLDIER *comes sweeping down along the front of the bar, pushing the* DRINKER *roughly out of his way.*

SOLDIER. Ho-ho –

LANDLORD. Now wait a minute, wait a minute . . .

SOLDIER (*waving a bottle in a wild attitude*).

> Ho-ho, boys, I'll tell yous.
> The noble battle-honours, my boys,
> Of the Caledonian Fusiliers.
> Serve every man a drink:
> There's all of my silver
> There on the timber!

(*The* LANDLORD *rather dubious. But as the company come forward with their empty glasses, murmuring gratefully, he begins to serve them all.*

*The* SOLDIER *has assumed a rhetorical attitude for his narration, though once or twice during it he breaks off and moves about the room, clapping people on the back and generally seizing their attention.)*

Nineteen thirty-nine:
I join with the regiment.
Ye'll remember, next year,
Beaches of Dunkirk;
We're against a Scots Guards company,
All fists and feet, boy . . .
Puts their CSM to hospital
And a Provost-Corporal no teeth left.
Every man a drink!
Nineteen forty-one, where were we then?
Catterick, och aye, the old Tank Corps
Twelve with broken ribs
And three for psychiatric treatment.
Six of our own boys
Northallerton Glasshouse.
Christmas forty-two,
Recapture of Tobruk,
The Australian fighting Army:
Never looked up after that day:
Chased 'em fifty miles.
Forty-three, Forty-four
Africa and Italy.
Matched against the Yanks
The most of that time.
They'd never a chance
With those rubber-soled boots, man.
We knew the game to give 'em.
And the Polack soldiers too.
*We* showed 'em where.
Polacks fought beside us once:
Against the Free French Navy:

Drowned them in dozens.

They used knives, the Polacks.

Then after the war . . .

PARKER (*thrusting forward*). After the war.

SOLDIER (*savagely*). I'm talking, mucker.

PARKER.

Aye, but after the war.

Were you ever in Germany?

SOLDIER.

Himmelherrgottkreuzmillionendonnerwetter!

Were *we* ever in Germany!

Who were the boys

Set Düsseldorf Naafi club on fire?

Who stole the Burgomaster's daughter

Out of Bacharach-on-Rhine?

There was a song made over that:

I'm going to sing it to yous.

Shut your mouths, every man.

(*He jumps up on to a table and begins to sing in a strong but not untuneable voice. Air: 'The Reformed Rake'.*)

'My father he told me

Never go with the soldiers,

Never go with the soldiers,

O my daughter dear.

I swore to obey him,

Little thought how this morning

I'd wake in the arms

Of my fine Fusilier.'

(*The* LANDLORD *is looking at his watch. Acknowledging applause*):

There was more verses, aye,

But they've gone from my mind.

LANDLORD. All right, it's Time, everybody, Time! Who can take a hint, eh? *Time* is what I said –

SOLDIER.
> So instead I'll play the tune to yous
> On my old tin whistle.

*He produces a penny whistle from his pocket.*

LANDLORD (*his hand on the light switches*). Half past ten. *I've* got the law to keep, soldier, whatever you may be thinking of doing.
(*The* SOLDIER *makes a rude noise at the* LANDLORD. *He plays the tune on his whistle, and performs a little step-dance on the table.*)
All right then. All right.

*The* LANDLORD *switches the lights out, leaving the room illuminated by the bar light only.*

SOLDIER (*violently*).
> All right then yourself then, mucker.
> Up the Fusiliers.

*He jumps down from the table, and sweeps a row of glasses to the floor with his arm.*
*Close-up of a bottle smashing into a mirror.*
*Shouting, running feet, police whistles. Silence.*


*The corner of a street.*
*The street is dark and empty, save for the* SOLDIER, *who leans against a lamp-post playing 'The Reformed Rake' on his whistle, and speaking to the moon between each line of the music.*

SOLDIER.
> I've missed my train to Aldershot . . . (*Music*)
> No money for a bed . . . (*Music*)
> I hit a yelping polisman . . . (*Music*)
> With a bottle on the head.

Am I no a dandy travelling soldier?

I cannot even tell ye the name of this town.

PARKER (*from off-screen*).

Well it's not Folkestone nor Dover.

And it's not Inverness, Serjeant,

I can tell you that's true.

PARKER *comes forward out of the shadows. The* SOLDIER *looks at him sardonically.*

SOLDIER. And *you're* not my Uncle Alexander and I'm not a Minister of the Free Kirk and who the hell are ye anyway?

PARKER. My name's Parker, Serjeant.

SOLDIER. Indeed. Nosey Parker, I dare well say.

PARKER. There's no call for discourtesy, you know. I did you a favour getting you out of that public.

SOLDIER. Awa' with your favours.

PARKER. Now then, now then . . .

SOLDIER. I am seeking my own society the night. I need no man's favourings.

PARKER. You've missed your train to Aldershot; there's not another while morning. What'll they do to you when you get there a day late?

SOLDIER (*matter-of-fact*). The usual, they'll do. 'Cap and belt off, witness – accused – escort 'tenshun, left turn, right turn, quick-march leftright leftright leftright, left wheel right wheel, mark time leftright leftright leftright . . . Halt!' 'Twenty-four hours absent without leave have you anything to say?' 'Permission to speak, sir? Nothing to say, sir.' 'How many more times are you going to be brought up before me on this sort of charge, most unsatisfactory, seven days detention three days loss of pay Royal Warrant, march him out, Sarnt-major.' 'Seven days detention three days Royal Warrant leftright leftright leftright . . . Halt!' God send us all good ending.

PARKER (*extremely impressed*). It's wicked, it's right wicked any lad should suffer that.

SOLDIER. A very honest opinion, mucker. Vastly does ye credit.

*The* SOLDIER *starts to play on his whistle again, clearly wishing to be rid of the other.*
*PARKER dithers about for a moment, then decides to reopen the conversation.*

PARKER. You, er – got anywhere to stay tonight?

SOLDIER. Not that I know.

PARKER. There's no question of your not having enough to pay for a bed, though, is there?

SOLDIER. Is there? Isn't there? What makes ye imagine that?

PARKER (*insinuating*). Well now, Serjeant, I saw all that brass you was broadcasting out on bar counter. I'm not blind.

SOLDIER (*sharply*). No? But ye're no so perspicacious, I dare venture, as to look clear into the pooches of a man's breeks, and reckon precisely just what silver remains there, hey?
(*He puts his hand in his trews pocket and pulls out a few coins, which he holds out for* PARKER'S *inspection.*)
Two shillings and fivepence ha'penny, and what the devil is it to you?

PARKER (*suddenly*). Do you know Tommy Scuffham?

SOLDIER (*carelessly*). I do not.

PARKER. Not in Germany?

SOLDIER. Never heard of him.

PARKER (*rather dashed*). Eh, dear . . .

SOLDIER. What d'ye mean. 'Eh, dear'?

PARKER. Now look, Serjeant, I'm not a military man, you know . . .

SOLDIER. I'll believe that.

PARKER. Indeed, I'd go so far as to say as my principles don't hold with the Army . . . er, that's not personal you know, no offence, no offence. We all have our views, don't we, entitled to our own views, but you, er – ah the fact is –

(*The* SOLDIER *walks away from him, but* PARKER *trots round in front and prevents his escape.*)

You see, Charlie Scuffham he cleans the windows, he's a very old friend of mine. Aye, and his wife, too, our Ida, that is, Ida Scuffham, you know . . .

SOLDIER (*sings: tune as before*).

'My father he told me
If you go with the soldiers
They'll lead you a journey
Of sin and of shame . . .'

PARKER. And it's over two years now since they heard a single word of him – well, I mean they're fair worried about it, bound to be, it's only nature, isn't it?

SOLDIER (*sings*).

'And if I go back to
The house where they reared me,
How can I face up
To such merited blame?'

PARKER (*still pursuing*). You see I thought – like – this Tommy Scuffham, if you'd ever heard of him, if you'd heard a word of him and you told them about it, his mum and dad and Mary, you know – I mean you're in same regiment, after all, I thought you might have known . . .

SOLDIER (*vaguely*). Regiment, whose regiment? . . .

(*The* SOLDIER *ponders a moment, looking at* PARKER *as though he has not heard what he has been saying until this minute. He leans against a doorway, looking up to the sky, and appears to reminisce.*)

Johnny Scruff – Och aye, Johnny Scuffham. God, he was the boy.

PARKER (*gently*). Tommy Scuffham.

SOLDIER (*carelessly*). Och aye, Tommy. We always called him Johnny. God, he was the boy.

PARKER. Aye, but what's happened to him, that's what we
. . .

SOLDIER (*mysteriously*). Happened to him? Aha – *there's* a question, mucker.

PARKER. Aye, but . . .

SOLDIER. *There* is a question . . . Mary?

PARKER. That's right. She's his wife.

SOLDIER. Will *I* put a question to *you* then? Have *you* got a wife?

PARKER (*taken aback*). Me?

SOLDIER. You.

PARKER. I've got a wife.

SOLDIER (*clapping him on the shoulder*). Then ye're a marvellous man, mucker. Lead me to her.

PARKER (*even more taken aback*). My wife?

SOLDIER (*cheerfully*). Och no. Tommy's wife, Johnny's Mary, mum, dad, and the kailyard cock. That's a very interesting question ye put: what's happened to Johnny. Tommy?

PARKER. Tommy.

SOLDIER. Ha!

*The* SOLDIER *plays 'Soldier, Soldier' on his whistle, and the two of them march off down the deserted street.*


MARY'S *bedroom, in the* SCUFFHAMS' *house.*
*Close-up of a toy soldier on a chair, and a pair of hands playing with it.*
*They are* MARY'S *hands, and we now see her face. During this scene her whole person and the room are gradually revealed. She is a girl in her early twenties, tidily yet dowdily dressed. Her general appearance is rather slow and cow-like – an impression belied by the intensity of her eyes. She is not a big girl, but her movements are gauche and self-conscious.*
*She is lying stretched out on her stomach on an ugly brass bedstead. The other furniture in the little room consists of a wash-stand with jug and basin and a chest of drawers. The room is untidy*

*and littered with clothes, etc., but the chest of drawers has nothing on top of it save a cheap plaster statue of the madonna and child and a little bowl of flowers in front. It is after dark and the naked electric bulb in the ceiling is lit.*

MARY (*sings quietly. Air: 'Soldier, Soldier'*).

> 'O Soldier, Soldier,
> Will you marry me now,
> With a hey and a ho
> And a fife and a drum . . .'

CHARLIE SCUFFHAM'S VOICE (*from off-screen*). Mary . . . Mary! Have you gone to bed, Mary?
(*She makes no sign of having heard him, although she stops singing to herself.*)
(*Off-screen, calling louder.*) I say have you gone to bed? There's Mrs Parker just come visiting. I say Mrs Parker's here to see you, Mary: are you coming down? Mary!

*With a sudden blow she sweeps her soldier on to the floor.*


*The living-kitchen.*
*This is a large room opening direct on to the street. It contains a kitchen range, table, chairs, sideboard, etc., and is somewhat over-crowded. The window looks out into the dark street beside the front door. In the back wall of the room, opposite the front door, are two other doors: one leading into a scullery-wash-house, and the other to the base of the stairs.*
CHARLIE SCUFFHAM *stands at the stair door, calling upwards. He is about sixty, in braces and shirtsleeves – a long lantern-jawed man, melancholy, and wears steel-rimmed spectacles.*

SCUFFHAM. Mary!
(*He turns back into the room, to confront his wife and* MRS PARKER. MRS SCUFFHAM *is a large slatternly sentimental*

*woman with a generally bothered air. Her friend is angular and sharp of speech, with a certain malicious quality of mind. She is the smarter dressed of the pair, and carries a handbag.)* She's not coming down.

MRS PARKER. Gone to bed, has she?

SCUFFHAM. Gone to her room.

MRS PARKER (*significantly*). Ah.

MRS SCUFFHAM. She's perhaps feeling poorly, poor love. She didn't eat her tea.

SCUFFHAM (*sharply*). She never eats her tea.

MRS SCUFFHAM (*injured*). Well, it wor a lovely tea, I made her a lovely tea. There was chips from around the corner, and a bit of pork-pie fried, and treacle we had, and a lovely yellow cake bought special, and she wouldn't take a bite. It's downright criminal, all that good shop food goes to waste. Of course, she thinks on Tommy, all the time.

MRS PARKER. Well, she's only herself to thank for that.

MRS SCUFFHAM (*vaguely compassionate*). She wor always very fond of our Tommy.

SCUFFHAM (*bitterly*). Mrs Parker's right. She's only herself to thank. Them as takes up sword has to perish by sword. When he went for a Regular soldier, he threw up everything I tried to learn him. It's what your husband says, Mrs Parker, Force and Colonialism: that's how he stands now: and strike-breaking and all that. I ask you, is it surprising he got married to . . .

*He gestures contemptuously upstairs.*

MRS PARKER. Irish, they said she was.

SCUFFHAM (*darkly*). Aye, but *we* reckon there's more to it than that, you know.

MRS SCUFFHAM. Many's the time I've looked at her and wondered.

MRS PARKER (*producing a bundle of tracts*). I thought I'd bring these for her tonight, but if she's gone up to bed . . .

MRS SCUFFHAM (*more to herself than otherwise*). His first leave from the Army, 'Hello, Mum,' he says – 'What do you think of the uniform, Scotch tartan and all – and what do you think of my Mary: we got married last week,' he says. His first leave – 'We got married last week,' he says.

MRS PARKER. It's – like – half a dozen tracts I got from Chapel, if she could be brought to have a read of them –

MRS SCUFFHAM. His first leave it was: he fetches her home, he took her and put her upstairs in the little bedroom, next morning he goes off to Germany and we never hear a word of him since.

SCUFFHAM. She won't read them, Mrs Parker, and that's nowt but bare truth. I've talked myself into lockjaw telling her about the Wrath to Come and where she'll end up if she goes on and where has it got me?

MRS PARKER. She never comes to Chapel.

MRS SCUFFHAM (*mournfully*). I don't understand it. We've tried to get her to change and to go for *proper* religion, but . . .

SCUFFHAM (*hopelessly*). It's – like – Irish, you see, that's what they say she is.

*Someone knocks loudly on the street door. As they turn towards the door, the lower sash of the window is thrust up from outside and the* SOLDIER'S *head appears.*

SOLDIER. Are you at home? There's someone knocking at your door.

SCUFFHAM (*almost too astonished to speak*). Here, who do you think you are . . .

*More knocking.*

SOLDIER. Well, have ye no mind to see who it is?

MRS PARKER *opens the front door, very dubiously. Her husband is revealed on the step. At the sight of his wife he looks a little sheepish.*

PARKER. It's all right, Alice, it's me.

MRS PARKER (*dour*). Why?

SCUFFHAM. Hello, Joe. But who . . .

PARKER (*coming in, and indicating* SOLDIER). I met him down the road. I brought him along. Aldershot he ought to be at, but he was misdirected – like.

*MRS PARKER shuts the door.*

SOLDIER. 'Cause of inadequate co-ordination between supply and demand: What d'ye lack, mucker? We havena got it. What, not a sandwich? No! Do ye intend to invite me inside, or are we to be acquainted only through the window like a dram sold after hours? Because it's a piece cold on this pavement-stone.

PARKER. Oh, come in, come in, Serjeant.

(*He goes to open the door. Before he does so he turns and whispers confidentially to the others.*)

Call him Serjeant when he's in – he's not the softest feller to talk to, but he's worth it, you know.

(*He opens the door, and brings in the* SOLDIER. *Very genial.*)

Well, here he is. Serjeant, meet them all: here's Charlie Scuffham and here's our Ida, and this here's . . .

SOLDIER (*with appalling gallantry*). Ye do not need to tell me. She has the very flare and splendour of your nostrils, man. She is your own most faithful wife or I catch badgers in the moonlight. Mistress Parker, your continual health is my eternal solace. And the same to the lot of yous.

*He sits down in* SCUFFHAM'S *armchair, sprawls out his legs and stares at the ceiling.*

SCUFFHAM. Now, look here, Joe, what's all this about . . .

MRS SCUFFHAM. Who does he think he is, marching into our house?

MRS PARKER. I hope you've some reason for all this, Joe Parker . . .

(*Together.*)

*When they realize they are all talking at once they break off in embarrassment. There is a pause, then they all speak at once again.*

SCUFFHAM. But what . . . ⎫
MRS SCUFFHAM. Who . . . ⎬ (*Together.*)
MRS PARKER. I say . . . ⎭

*Another awkward pause.*

PARKER (*very significantly*). Caledonian Fusiliers.
SCUFFHAM. Caledonian . . .
MRS SCUFFHAM. Caledonian . . .
MRS PARKER. Oh. Oh.

*It sinks in, and they speak one after another in great hurry.*

SCUFFHAM. Do you mean to say . . .
MRS SCUFFHAM. You mean to say he *knows* summat . . .
SCUFFHAM. Summat of that lad . . .
MRS SCUFFHAM. Our Tommy, he's not got word of our Tommy?

*They all look at the* SOLDIER, *who appears to have gone to sleep. At length he realizes that this is his cue.*

SOLDIER. Ah, he was the boy. Johnny.
PARKER. Tommy.
SOLDIER (*pulling himself together*).
 Scuffham. Ach, he was the boy.
 Tommy Scuffham. *I* was there, aye,
 The day they threw him inside:
 It's at gate of the camp, ye see,
 Half past twelve is midnight,
 Here he comes, wee Tommy,
 Dancing like an ostrich,
 Hooting stinking drunk,
 And five of these Kraut women,

Bully brawney ten-ton Frauleins . . .
They comb their hair with razors, those!
So here's Big McCluskey,
Serjeant of the Guard
Who goes there, he says.
Friend, says wee Tommy.
Man, I'm no a man
To kick the teeth in of a friend,
So he kicks him in the wame.

SCUFFHAM. Who kicks who?

SOLDIER. He kicks him.

SCUFFHAM. Who?

SOLDIER. Why, Big McCluskey, who else?

MRS SCUFFHAM (*in horror*). He kicks our Tommy . . .

SOLDIER.

Na na na,
How the devil can he,
He's bang on his back in the road
Flatter than a cowpat
And (God he's the boy)
He sets his bully foot
Plank on his thick red neck:
Hoot, he says, I've killed him.

PARKER (*bewildered*). Tommy Scuffham killed him? He went
and killed a Serjeant!

SOLDIER. Have I not just said so? Ye're all as deaf as white
herrings. Mphm.

PARKER. But – but – what happened?

SOLDIER. Happened when?

PARKER. Well happened to Tommy, after all that.

SOLDIER. Och aye, to Tommy. Aye well, what happened?
Well, what d'ye think *should* happen? They threw him
inside.

MRS SCUFFHAM (*tremulously*). Inside?

SOLDIER. Aye. I doubt he's still there.

MRS SCUFFHAM. Not – not in . . .

SCUFFHAM. You don't mean he's gone to *prison*?

SOLDIER. Where else would he go? Aye, aye, the glasshouse. He broke McCluskey's jaw – put him off duty three months. I told ye, quite killed.

*They all sit stunned.*

MRS PARKER (*savouring the situation*). Eh, think of that now. Prison.

MARY'S *bedroom.*

*She is sitting cross-legged on her bed, tying knots in a woven belt of the Irish type. Her soldier lies where she has left it in the previous scene.*

MARY (*in a crooning voice as though repeating a nursery rhyme or a charm*).

One year comes and turns its back.

(*Ties knot.*)

Two years comes and turns its back.

(*Ties knot.*)

Three years coming.

(*Begins third knot, but leaves it loose.*)

How to speak

Words of life are white or black

But how should I know how to speak?

For live words now this jaw would break.

*The* SOLDIER'S *whistle is heard off; playing 'Soldier, Soldier'. She stiffens into attention, then gets up from the bed, goes to the door to listen, and hums the tune herself in company with his music.*

SOLDIER (*calling from off-screen*). Mary, is it Mary, Tommy's Mary? Oo hoo hoo!

*She pulls the third knot tight.*

MARY (*to herself*). Three years coming. How to speak.

*She turns the handle of the door to open it.*

*The stairs seen from a point about half-way down.*
*The door of* MARY'S *room is, as it were, above and behind the camera, which is looking down at the* SOLDIER, *who has come out of the living-kitchen and is starting to climb.*

SOLDIER. Oo hoo hoo – Mary.

MARY (*off-screen*). Who are you? What do you want?

SOLDIER (*easily*). Not a thing more than one sandwich, egg, cheese, or meat.

MRS SCUFFHAM *appears at the bottom of the stairs behind the* SOLDIER.

MRS SCUFFHAM. Come down, Mary, do. He's brought us word of Tommy.

SOLDIER. Ach, he was the boy.

MARY (*coming into the camera range*).
    If it's only a sandwich, mister,
    It'll not take a minute to make.

*The street containing the* SCUFFHAMS' *house. A typical street in a colliery town, with houses of black brick or stone, stone-sett paving, a general air of muck without much money. It is Sunday morning. Church bells are ringing.* CHARLIE SCUFFHAM *appears at his front door, in shirtsleeves as before. He walks across the street to a little newsagent's shop, from which he almost immediately reappears with a number of newspapers. He glances doubtfully at the front pages of these, then re-enters his house, picking up a milk bottle on the way in.*

*The living-kitchen.*

CHARLIE SCUFFHAM *comes in from the street, puts his milk and papers down on the table, and studies the papers with an increasing frown. They are all journals of the sex-and-scandal variety with pin-up photographs much in evidence.* MARY *is beside the kitchen range, arranging a breakfast tray. The room is in a very untidy state, as before; but this is increased by the fact that there has been a bed made up on an uncomfortable arrangement of chairs and sofa in one corner.* MARY *turns away from the range, about to carry her tray upstairs.*

SCUFFHAM (*sharply*). What's all that you're carrying?

MARY (*dully*). Breakfast, that's what.

SCUFFHAM. Who for?

MARY. Himself upstairs. In your bedroom.

SCUFFHAM(*fussily*). Well, make sure you give him right plenty. How many eggs? Two? He could eat three, you know; he's a big strong-set man . . .

MARY. There's no more than two in the house. Oo, it's a lot for him, is two.

SCUFFHAM (*handing her all the newspapers*). Here's his Sunday papers like he said; now you take 'em up.

MARY. I will. Are you wanting a look at them, Mr Scuffham, first?

SCUFFHAM (*shocked*). Indeed I'm not. Now, is there owt else he'd like? Must make sure he gets everything he'd like . . .

MARY (*muttering into the breakfast tray*). How about a hug and a kiss of your own wife, or maybe a . . .

SCUFFHAM (*very angry, but not quite sure he heard*). What did you say! Now, you look here, I'm telling you . . .

MRS SCUFFHAM *is seen appearing at the scullery door.*

MRS SCUFFHAM. You take that tray up to the Serjeant, Mary,

and don't talk back to your dad. You ought to show a sight more grateful, you ought, all the help he's going to give us for poor Tommy in his trouble.

MARY (*quietly*). I'm sorry indeed. Of course, it's quite right we should look after the Serjeant for whatever length of time he's wanting to stay.

MARY *goes upstairs with the tray.* MRS SCUFFHAM *starts tidying the makeshift bed in a half-hearted sort of fashion.*

MRS SCUFFHAM. Well, it *is* a length of time, you know, choose what. After all, it'll be near on for a week . . .

SCUFFHAM (*firmly*). Joe Parker says we've to let him lie.

MRS SCUFFHAM (*crossly*). Oh, Joe Parker . . .

SCUFFHAM (*convincing himself as much as her*). Say he goes back to barracks: they run him in – he's overstayed his leave. What sort of help can he do for our Tommy's trouble then ?

MRS SCUFFHAM (*still doubtful*). That's what Joe says.

SCUFFHAM. Aye. But *I* don't know: all them magazine-books he wants, and Sunday papers, too.

MRS SCUFFHAM. I wish I could follow what Joe Parker was after.

SCUFFHAM (*pursuing his own line of thought*). Bare women and that. It's not what I'm used to.

MRS SCUFFHAM. How much money does that Serjeant reckon we'll need ?

SCUFFHAM. Are we going to chapel ? No, Joe might come round.

MRS SCUFFHAM. I think I'll go. I feel that upset, a bit of hymn-singing'd do me good maybe. I'll go with Alice Parker.

SCUFFHAM. Of course, some of them are wearing – like – camisoles and bathing-dresses: aye. Never mind for money. *We'll* pay what's needful.

MRS SCUFFHAM. Army or no Army, Tommy's our lad, he's our boy.

*The* SCUFFHAMS' *bedroom.*
*This room is rather larger than* MARY'S, *but is furnished in similar style. It has a brass double bed, in which the* SOLDIER *is seated, very much at ease, eating his breakfast and studying the Sunday papers. He is wearing his underclothing.* MARY *stands beside the bed and watches him eat.*

MARY (*rather unfriendly*). There's two eggs for you. There's fried bacon, there's toasted bread and marge and jam. They'll not be giving Tommy Scuffham that in the prison.

SOLDIER (*speaking laconically between mouthfuls*). A half-piece stale bread, a cat's-claw lard, a drain-and-a-quarter bracken-water and that they call it tea. 'Any complaints?' 'No complaints, sir.' 'Prisoners, carry on.'

MARY. Justly or unjustly there?

SOLDIER (*pointing out a photo in his paper*).

    Will ye take a look at *her*,
    There's a lifty leg
    Ye could get between ten fingers,
    There's a rump-end for ye . . .
    Full moon over Sandy's haystack, hey?
    Unjustly, what else?
    Did I not make it clear:
    Whatever poor dog of a soldier
    Went *justly* to the jail?

MARY.

    But the two of them below there,
    All that money they're after gathering,
    How will that help?

SOLDIER (*like a cross-examining counsel*).

    Is he or is he not
    To have a retrial?

MARY.

> That's your advice, indeed,
> Why shouldn't it be good?

SOLDIER.

> And how can he have a retrial
> Without there's new evidence?

MARY (*considering slowly*).

> Sure that was your point of view.
> Truly, truly . . .

SOLDIER.

> And how can ye get evidence
> Without that ye pay for it?
> Is he in Germany? He is.
> And what like are the German women?

MARY (*carefully repeating what she has heard*).

> Swear away their grandpas' lives
> For the price of a fish-hook.

SOLDIER (*in some astonishment*).

> That's what I told ye.
> Ye remember it well.

(*He points to another photo in the paper.*)

> Ye see her, lassie, ye see her?
> Now what would ye say
> She was wearing under that sweater?
> Ye'll never make me believe
> That's her own unaided effort.

MARY (*with an unexpected satirical smile, her first*).

> His Mum and Dad, you know,
> I'll tell you what I think there:
> I think they're nothing but a pair
> Of washbowls on the waves of ocean,
> They've not I think between them
> Got one notion.

SOLDIER (*acutely*). And who *has* got the one notion?

MARY (*serious again*).

Yourself maybe, why not?
Or what about Joe Parker.
SOLDIER.
Aha there, he's the boy.
Nosey knows
What Nosey ought to know.
Give him the money,
Says Nosey Joe.
Now why?
MARY. He's a good friend of Charlie Scuffham.

*The* SOLDIER, *having finished his breakfast, pushes the tray away, lays down his newspapers, and gives* MARY *a considering look.*

SOLDIER. And I was a good friend of your Tommy's, was I no? Ach, he says to me one time: 'You ever go to England, mucker, and ye'll stand in the road and ye'll see her come toward ye, and tripping her legs together like the tick-tock of a clock, and she carries her wee belly like the flourishing colours of the regiment, and her brisk bosom, mucker, is a bugle. And then, mucker,' he says, 'ye'll be looking at my wife.' He says that to me.
MARY (*round-eyed*). Truly?
SOLDIER. Aye, truly.
MARY. In Germany, why not.

*There is a knocking at the front door, off.*

PARKER (*off-screen*). Hello, Charlie, are you in?
SOLDIER. Do we hear Nosey Parker down the stairs?
MARY. I've got to go now, else I'd be late.
(*She walks to the door, then stops, considers, looks at her legs and up at the* SOLDIER *again, with her smile briefly reappearing.*)
Tick-tock, like a clock?

SOLDIER. Tick-tock.

*He makes a noise like a bugle.*

*The living-kitchen.*

SCUFFHAM, *alone in the room, opens the door and admits* PARKER.

SCUFFHAM. Come in, Joe, come in. I were just waiting on you. Ida's gone to chapel.

PARKER (*coming in*). Aye. With my Alice. I tell you, Charlie, I could do with a . . .

*He makes a gesture suggestive of pouring out and swallowing a drink.*

SCUFFHAM (*sternly*). No, Joe, it wouldn't be right. 'Strong drink is raging.'

PARKER. Not in this house it never is.

(MARY *comes in from the stairs, putting on a headscarf. She walks across the room and goes out into the street.*)

Where's *she* off to so swift and airy?

SCUFFHAM (*sourly*). Babylon.

PARKER. Where?

SCUFFHAM. House of Rimmon. No two words for it.

PARKER. How's she been taking the news?

SCUFFHAM. Why, you can't say she's been taking it at all. No effect at all. It fair beats me.

PARKER. Ah . . . I'll tell you what's beating *me*, Charlie, and it's this: if your lad was into an Army jail, why warn't you notified? Next of kin, you know. Or else Mary is, choose what. *She* should have been told.

SCUFFHAM. Maybe we were told. I don't know.

PARKER. What do you mean, you don't know?

SCUFFHAM (*resentfully*). Well, we get these letters, you see.

One month or another month we'll get 'em. Majesty's Service. *I* don't read 'em.

PARKER. Why not?

SCUFFHAM. Well it's not right to trouble a man with that sort of thing. I've got better thoughts to bother with. And Ida don't read 'em either. Why should she? It's only – like – Government Propaganda.

PARKER. Aye, that's a point there. What about Mary?

SCUFFHAM. Oh, *she* don't get no letters.

PARKER. Any Army marriage allowance?

SCUFFHAM. No. I don't reckon our Tommy can have told about her to the Army. Why should he? It's nowt to do with them.

PARKER (*sitting comfortable at the table*). Now look here, Charlie, I've been settling my mind on to this business for a good long while. And this is what it seems to me. Tabulated conclusion: One: Your lad's been put in jail for summat he didn't do or if he *did* do there was extenuating circumstances as was not yet fully brought out. Two: In order to bring them out we are entirely dependent on the good nature of that feller upstairs and you've got to find the money yourself to pay for the witnesses. Three: It can't have been a fair trial if all that is like it is. Four: Why didn't the Army tell you? You say you might have had letters: so what? Because *I* say, Five: It's their business to make sure you *read* 'em. All right, so what does it add up to?

SCUFFHAM (*thinking carefully*). Well, to my way of thought, Joe, it is not all what I'd call democracy. That's right, isn't it?

PARKER. That's right. And I'm going to make a fair commotion about it and all, I'm telling you. There's council elections next month. You know I'm standing, don't you?

SCUFFHAM. Aye. Aye, I know.

PARKER. Aye, well. Here's my platform: ledged, braced, and battened for me. You've always heard my views about jack-booted militarism. Here is the proof.

*The* SOLDIER *off-screen. Sings. Air: 'Onward Christian Soldiers'.*

SOLDIER.

'Lloyd George knew my father,
My father knew Lloyd George . . .'

(*The* SOLDIER *enters from the stairs in vest and trews, brandishing a cut-throat razor and a shaving-brush.*)

I'm awa' into the scullery for a shave. Which one of yous has any objections?

SCUFFHAM (*nervously*). No – no one of us at all, Serjeant; you carry on. You know where the towel is and the piece of soap, don't you? I wor just going to have a bit of a rinse, myself, but . . .

*The* SOLDIER *goes into the scullery, singing as before. The other two continue their conversation in abated tones.*

PARKER. Jackbooted militarism. Do you know what that poor lad told me, Charlie? The things that they're going to do to him when he gets back from being late off leave? Fair makes your blood run cold. And for why? 'Cause he missed his train, that's all.

*The* SOLDIER *sticks a belathered face round the scullery door.*

SOLDIER. Ye know, I'll tell ye a thing, Mr Parker. All women in this world is divided into the two kinds. There's Birds, and there's Puddings. Now of what kind would ye imagine is you wife, man?

PARKER. Eh, I don't know.

SOLDIER. Bird. All sinews and claw feet with a wee bit beak at the north end.

*He goes back into the scullery.*

PARKER. Now, that's what I like about that feller. Despite it all in the circumstances of his degraded way of life, he still keeps live and smiling.

*The* SOLDIER *reappears, using the razor.*

SOLDIER. Mistress *Scuffham*: ha! She is, without doubt, a Pudding. There was something of a deficiency in the baking-powder, fell a piece sodden in the oven, did it no? But let that rest. They tell me, Mr Parker, that ye are a sort of a politician. Do ye ken what they think of politicians in the Army?

PARKER. Can't say as I do.

SOLDIER. I'll whisper it. I doubt Mr Scuffham wouldna care to hear it aloud.

*He whispers in* PARKER'S *ear.* PARKER *jumps to his feet angrily.*

PARKER. Now, you look here, a joke's a joke . . .

SOLDIER. I'll not deny that, mucker.

*They glare at each other for a moment. Then* PARKER *thinks the better of it and sits down again.*

PARKER. Well, all right, all right, no offence taken.

SCUFFHAM (*anxiously changing the subject*). About that money, Serjeant. We're getting it together, by degrees – like. About how much do you reckon we'll need?

SOLDIER (*cruelly casual*). I wouldna like to say . . . Anything less of fifty they'll spit in your gob.

SCUFFHAM. Eh dear. We can maybe make forty-five if we take out Ida's Post Office . . .

SOLDIER (*helping himself to a draught from the milk bottle*). There's one variety of a woman, ye do not commonly meet her, she is able to combine the qualities both of Bird and of Pudding. She has the wee nervousness of the one and the warmth and fullness of the other. Rare; desirable; she'll load ye down to death.

PARKER. She seems a kind of a pigeon-pie, eh? Heh heh.

SOLDIER. Mphm.

*He goes back into the scullery.*

PARKER. What I've been thinking, Charlie, you see, not only your Tommy, but *him* as well.

SCUFFHAM. Him?

PARKER. Victim. Jackboots; so forth, so forth. Very good material for a platform, that lad. All them tales he tells . . . why, do you know what he says some of the Army was doing in West Germany a year or two since?

SCUFFHAM. I was here when he told. Fair shocking, warn't it?

PARKER. You see the line, eh? Connived at by Government – like – excesses of military power. Etcetera, so forth. I think he'd do it, you know. And another thing. He's missed his ten-o'clock train. So he might as well stay. What about it?

SCUFFHAM. I don't know . . .

PARKER (*calling*). Serjeant?

SOLDIER (*from inside the scullery*). Hello there!

PARKER. Speaking quite frank, Serjeant, from the shoulder, no holds barred: what is your opinion of the Army?

*There is a pause. The* SOLDIER *comes out of the scullery, shaved.*

SOLDIER. Will ye ask that again?

PARKER. What is your opinion of the Army?

SOLDIER. I think I'd best to whisper *that* one, too.

*He comes forward again to* PARKER'S *ear, but* PARKER *gets up and forestalls him with a triumphant smile.*

PARKER. Say no more, Serjeant, say no more. You've told me all I want to know.

*The exterior of a typical Nonconformist chapel, very hard, unsympathetic architecture.*
*Sounds of congregation inside concluding a hymn with a vigorous 'Amen'.*

MRS SCUFFHAM *and* MRS PARKER *come out, before the singing stops.*

*The chapel porch.*
MRS SCUFFHAM *and* MRS PARKER *walk away from the doorway towards a seat set along the chapel wall in the sunshine. Another hymn begins in the chapel.*

MRS PARKER (*sympathetically*). Come along here, love, there's a seat. There you are now.
(*She helps* MRS SCUFFHAM *to sit down, and sits down herself.*)
Are you still feeling poorly?

MRS SCUFFHAM. No. No, I'm a bit better now, Alice, now that I've got out into fresh air. It wor just one of my turns, you know. I think it's all this hot weather. Charlie Scuffham reckons it's the atom bombs they . . .

MRS PARKER. Now, don't try and talk so much, love. Just you sit quiet.

MRS SCUFFHAM. It's near on a week now, Alice, and he wants all our savings . . . well, *I* don't know – your Joe says it's all right, it wor Joe brought him after all, and . . . I don't see how our Tommy could ever have done all them dreadful things . . . (*She starts to cry, and fumbles for her handkerchief.*) It's not right they should just lock him up and never let us know. And what about Mary, that's what I say, Alice – what are we to do?

MRS PARKER (*sagely*). Ah, there'll be a strain there, I'll be bound.

MRS SCUFFHAM. If she could only cry a bit – like – it would be better for her, wouldn't it? I say to her, 'It'll do you good', but she won't take notice: I say to her, 'Have a good cry with me, love', but – but she doesn't seem to want to.

MRS PARKER (*censorious*). It's what they want you never know,

that sort. You take Ethel Hopkins for an instance. Her boy,
you know, he was in the Air Force in the war, and he went
and he got married in Southampton . . . well, I *mean* . . .

MRS SCUFFHAM. Eh dear. Southampton.

MRS PARKER. He brought her home and the next thing he
knew she was off to Scarborough with his own brother.

MRS SCUFFHAM. What, him as worked down pit?

MRS PARKER. Aye. That one. She used to sing him a song
about it – (*She breaks off and looks sharply down the street.*)
Look.

(*The view down the street as seen from the chapel porch.* MARY
*is walking briskly along on her way home from mass. As we watch
her we hear the conversation of the other two women continuing.*)
A terrible song she used to sing:

(*She renders it in a queer high-pitched chant.*)

> 'Collier-boys gets gold and silver
> Aircraftmen gets nowt but brass:
> I'm away with a bonny collier
> For to be his dancing lass.'

Ethel told me she heard her sing that under her husband's
very nose. Aye, and dancing at him, too.

MARY *walks past the chapel without paying them any attention.*
MRS PARKER *and* MRS SCUFFHAM *watch* MARY *out of
sight.*

MRS SCUFFHAM (*suddenly catching the allusion*). Eh, but,
Alice, you don't think . . .

MRS PARKER (*judiciously*). Of course a collier's not a Serjeant,
nor a Serjeant's not a collier.

MRS SCUFFHAM (*very troubled*). Charlie Scuffham says your
Joe says he's not a right Serjeant at all.

MRS PARKER (*gloating*). I know. Only making it worse, you
see.

MRS SCUFFHAM. Eh dear, I never thought of it *that* way. What are we going to do?

MRS PARKER. There's not much you can do, Ida, except keep a sharp eye.

MRS SCUFFHAM. And that's what I'll do, and all. I'll tell you, Alice, I'll do it.

MRS PARKER. Aye, and I'll help you.

MRS SCUFFHAM (*very determined*). I'll do it.

MRS PARKER. I'll do it, too.

*The street containing the* SCUFFHAMS' *house.* MARY *comes up the street and enters the front door.*

*The living-kitchen.*

MARY *enters from the street. She stands just inside the door, astonished at what she sees. What she sees is* PARKER *performing a step-dance on the table among a litter of beer bottles, and the* SOLDIER *sprawling (by now fully dressed) in a chair, whistling a jig on his penny-whistle.* SCUFFHAM *is nowhere to be seen. When* PARKER *realizes* MARY *is in the room he stops dancing and climbs down, a trifle embarrassed.*

PARKER. I was just, er – recollecting, as you might have it, er – like – accomplishments of my youth. Heh.

SOLDIER (*appreciatively*).
        It's no so bad, mucker, mind ye,
        No so bad at all.
        Your old age cries up maybe
        From your knee-joints
        Like blood in the gutter,
        But for all that ye have movement.

MARY (*awestruck*). But where's Mr Scuffham?

SOLDIER (*playing a little twirl of music*).

He's in the back scullery.

He doesna approve.

No, says Charlie,

It's profanation of the Sabbath,

Says Charlie.

SCUFFHAM (*from inside the scullery*). It's a fair disgrace and no two words.

SOLDIER.

Ye hear?

The Demon Drink, is what.

And who's the man he had it brought?

Nosey Parker is the man:

*He* had it brought.

PARKER (*jovially*). Now, wait a minute, fair's fair . . .

MARY. That's a good quaint whistle you have there.

SOLDIER. It is.

MARY *and the* SOLDIER *stand looking one at the other for a moment.*

MARY (*on the spur of the moment*).

You can whistle me

And I will sing.

SOLDIER. What will you sing?

MARY.

Sure you must know it.

It's a very old tune

Derry down, down, down derry down.

PARKER. Eh, Mary, who'd have thought you sang?

MARY (*tartly*).

Supposing I do sing,

What is there wrong?

(*She turns away from* PARKER *and speaks earnestly and deliberately to the* SOLDIER.)

Tell me if this is not

A strong and proper song.

(*She starts to sing, in a fierce, harsh voice, giving more emphasis to the meaning of the words than to the music. The* SOLDIER *perches himself on the table-edge and accompanies her on the whistle, picking up the tune without difficulty. He joins raucously in the refrain at the end of each verse, as does* PARKER: *Air:* 'The Coal-Owner and the Pitman's Wife'.)

> 'I met my true love
> In the dark of the night:
> The old moon was dead
> And the new gave no light.
> I met my true love
> At the bottom of the town
> Where dark was the houses
> That cover the ground:
> Derry down, down, down derry down.'

SCUFFHAM *comes in from the scullery, black with anger.*

SCUFFHAM. Mary!

*No one takes any notice of him.*

MARY (*sings*).

> 'He says, "I'm a walking,
> Will you walk with me?
> I'm walking as far
> As the edge of the sea!"
> I followed him so
> Till he came to the strand
> And there a tall steamer
> Was sailing so grand:
> Derry down, down, down derry down.'

SCUFFHAM.

> Mary, I said, Mary!
> What sort of decent married wife
> Do you reckon *you're* acting
> On Lord's Day and all, what's next!

SOLDIER.

> Hold your holiness, mucker,
> She's singing us a song.

MARY (*sings*).

> ' "Oh now I must board her,"
> My true love did cry.
> "I'll come back and love you
> Again ere I die."
> Let him come back tomorrow
> Or in fifty year
> He's the last I will follow
> To Liverpool pier:
> Derry down, down, down derry down.'

*She triumphantly pours herself out a glass of beer and swallows it down. Meanwhile* MRS SCUFFHAM *and* MRS PARKER *have come in from the street and are standing aghast.*

SOLDIER.

> For Germany the steamers
> Sail out of Harwich.

MARY.

> That's what they told me
> After the marriage.

SCUFFHAM (*trembling with rage*).

> Marriage to a soldier
> Aye, to a soldier.

MRS PARKER (*very vindictive*).

> Well might she call herself
> Married to a soldier.

PARKER (*trying to smooth things over*).

> It's just a bit of a singsong – like –
> They're none so bad, you know, aren't soldiers,
> Only – like – principle behind them that's vicious . . .

MRS PARKER.

> Aye, and an Irish wife

Well might she call herself
Married to a soldier.

MRS SCUFFHAM (*tearfully*).

Married to our Tommy
I don't know what road to look,
Under our very roof, Alice,
I'm that capped with shame,
Married to a soldier.

SOLDIER (*challenging*).

And what is a soldier?
All right, *I'm* a soldier,
So what word is that worth!

MRS SCUFFHAM. Word of shame . . .

MRS PARKER. Aye, shame.

SCUFFHAM. And no two words.

SOLDIER (*with deep feeling*).

So there is the truth . . .
What word's worth then those soldiers
Lives married to a *whoor* . . .
How many weary soldiers
North, south, islands or desert,
They standing there
All in the thrown stones
Or the bombs or the Serjeants-Major:
And where stands their wives?
Lying on their back
In the backends of Birmingham:
That's where *my* wife stood.
I used to have a wife.
For a whole half-year in Africa
I never heard one word.
But the fat woman kept the bakery
Next door to our house,
*She* wrote, she said:
'I would never interfere', she wrote,

> 'But was two sailors or a Yankee
> Or a black bus-conductor . . .
> They came by night and they went by night
> And I thought you ought to know.'

PARKER. But wait a minute, Serjeant . . .

SOLDIER (*disregarding him*).

> 'I thought ye ought to know', she writes,
> And *what* does he know:
> That in that outlandish standing
> There he has to stand,
> Three years, five years,
> *Eighteen* years is me . . .

(*He suddenly breaks off and lurches toward the street door, picking up and putting on his bonnet as he talks: disgusted.*)

> Ach I tried to help yous,
> But what service does it work . . .
> Why don't I go to Cyprus,
> Live with Venus,
> Roll me over lovely Cyprus,
> Call me a Greek or a Turk . . .

*He goes out violently from the house and slams the door behind him. They all look at one another.*

MRS PARKER. Well, what was all that about?

PARKER. Birmingham?

SCUFFHAM. I've never been to Birmingham in my life.

MRS SCUFFHAM. Then what d'you reckon he . . .

SCUFFHAM.

> Shut your old fat face, will you,
> I'm fair fed up with the lot.

*There is a pause.* MRS SCUFFHAM *snivels.* MARY *goes to the window and looks out after the* SOLDIER.

PARKER. Who's going to call him back? (*Another pause.*) Well, somebody'll have to go.

MRS PARKER. What about your savings?
MRS SCUFFHAM. What about our Tommy.

*Another pause. Then* SCUFFHAM *and* PARKER *get up together.*

SCUFFHAM ⎫
PARKER ⎭ *(together).* I'll go and get him . . .

*They bump into one another on their ways to the door.* MARY
*is at the door before them.*

MARY *(wearily).*
> Don't trouble at all.
> I'm the one to go.
> I'll bring him back.

SCUFFHAM. Now, you listen to me . . .
MRS SCUFFHAM. I don't think she ought to go . . .
MRS PARKER. Ask for your trouble, ask it.
MARY.
> Well, I'm going and I'm going,
> And that's all about it.
> Good-bye.

*She goes out into the street.*

MRS PARKER *(to* MRS SCUFFHAM).
> Do I have to say owt more.
> Are you deaf as well as blind?

MRS SCUFFHAM. We mustn't let her go.
*(She runs to the door and out a pace or two into the street,
leaving the door open.* SCUFFHAM *starts out after her, and calls
from the doorway.)*
> Mary, you're to come back here!

SCUFFHAM. Mary, I said *Mary!*
*The* PARKERS *remain inside the room.*
PARKER.
> Leave her be, leave her be,
> She'll maybe bring him back.

*The pub.*
*The* LANDLORD *and the* DRINKER *of the second scene in conversation across the bar.*

LANDLORD. He must be off his nut.

DRINKER. Of course he's off his nut. He's fair balmy. Sticks his head through window, he says, 'Window-cleaner,' he says. 'I'm come to clean your windows.' Well, my missus she just looks at him. 'Windows,' she says. 'What do you mean windows – it's Sunday afternoon!' We was just setting down to us teas. Windows!

LANDLORD. Fair balmy.

DRINKER. And then he goes on about this soldier. 'Where's he gone with our lad's Mary?' he says. 'Where's the heathen devil gone!' he says. Then he puts his foot through window, so I gets up and knocks him off his ladder. Drive you to drink!

LANDLORD. It's old Nosey Parker, you know. Him and that Jock Fusilier as broke all my glasses. Nosey was in here an hour since. Had I seen his Serjeant? No, I'd not seen his flickering Serjeant again. Poor old Charlie Scuffham.

DRINKER. Jock Fusilier? If it's *that's* the soldier, I've seen him.

LANDLORD. What, this evening?

DRINKER. Aye, this evening. Down by canal. Back of Ellenroyd's glassworks.

LANDLORD. Where there's all them reeds and bushes?

DRINKER. Aye, in there among the old iron.

LANDLORD. Who was he with?

(*The* DRINKER *lays one finger slyly on his nose and leers.*)
Not with . . .

DRINKER (*cunning*). Ah, but I didn't see her, you see, so I'm not saying owt. Just a voice, you see, I could hear, but not so as to know.

LANDLORD (*salaciously*). Like – laughing, and that?

DRINKER (*very salaciously*). Aye . . . 'Stop it, I like it' – eh? Heh, heh, heh!

LANDLORD. Poor old Charlie Scuffham.

*The streets of the town, early morning, vehicles, people going to work. Factory buzzers.*

*The street containing the* SCUFFHAMS' *house.* SCUFFHAM *comes up the street wheeling a bicycle with a ladder and bucket. He has a rag bandaging his head and looks worn out. He leaves his bicycle in the street and goes into the house with his impedimenta.*

*The living-kitchen.*

SCUFFHAM *comes pushing through the door and carries his ladder and bucket across the room to dump them in the scullery.* MRS SCUFFHAM *is asleep in a chair, fully dressed. She wakes up.*

SCUFFHAM. Are they back yet?

MRS SCUFFHAM (*very angry*). Where've you been all night?

SCUFFHAM (*hopelessly*). Cleaning windows.

MRS SCUFFHAM. Have you gone mad?

SCUFFHAM. I thought I wor going. That's why I went out with this lot. I had to do summat, Sunday or no. It wor either work or drink.

MRS SCUFFHAM. Are you sure it warn't drink?

SCUFFHAM (*crossly*). Aye, I'm sure, and I wish it had been. Are they back or aren't they?

MRS SCUFFHAM. They aren't.

SCUFFHAM. Where's Joe Parker and his missus?

MRS SCUFFHAM. I don't know.

SCUFFHAM (*imitating her whine, savagely*). 'You don't know!' What is there you *do* know! Can't even bring up a young lad but you've to let him get hisself all embrangled with murdering soldiers and dancing delilahs and God knows what else. I tell you, I'm just about . . .

(MARY *comes in from the street. Her manner is quiet and self-possessed. She seems, however, to be suppressing some strong emotion.*)

Oh!

*He has forgotten about his bucket and ladder, which now encumber the room.*

MRS SCUFFHAM. So you've come home!

MARY. I have.

MRS SCUFFHAM. You go to your room, till I'm ready to talk to you . . .

SCUFFHAM. You set down there. I've summat to say to you . . .

MARY. One at a time, now. I've time for you both.

SCUFFHAM. I said set down there. I've summat . . .

MRS SCUFFHAM. She can go to her room, go to her room. I can't hardly bring myself to look her in the face . . .

SCUFFHAM (*storming*). Are you going to set down or not?

MRS SCUFFHAM (*half-hysterical*). She's to go to her room!

MARY. God help us!

(*Her eye lights on the* SOLDIER'S *tin whistle, which lies where he left it on the table. She picks it up thoughtfully.*)

I'll go to my room.

SCUFFHAM. No you don't . . .

MARY. I do, so!

*She goes up the stairs.* SCUFFHAM *calls after her.*

SCUFFHAM. Here, come back here! What have you done with that soldier?

MARY (*calling from up the stairs*). You might well ask, Mr Scuffham, you might well ask indeed.

SCUFFHAM. *I'll* bring her down, *I'll* find the truth . . .

(*There is a knock on the door. He has got tangled with his ladder, etc.*)

Who's that?

MRS SCUFFHAM. Maybe it's . . .

SCUFFHAM. Well, open it and see.

*MRS SCUFFHAM opens the door and PARKER comes in, very jovial.*

PARKER. Hello, hello, hello, is he back yet, is he back?

SCUFFHAM. No, he's not.

PARKER. Well, he's on his road. I've seen him just now, seen him in Prospect Street . . . (*He sits down and smacks his hands together.*) Now, you listen to me, Charlie. Everything's lovely, it's all arranged. Last night where do you think I've been. I've been to Trades Union Offices up Balaclava Road, and who's there? The Mayor's there.

MRS SCUFFHAM (*impressed*). What, Alderman Butterthwaite?

PARKER. Aye, Cheery Uncle Butterthwaite. Well, *you* know him, Charlie. He's more than just Mayor; he's like Napoleon in this wappentake – Council, committees, unions and all – and he says to me, 'Joe,' he says, 'Joe . . .'

SCUFFHAM (*also impressed*). He called you Joe!

PARKER. He called me Joe. He says, 'Joe, that soldier's worth a mine of black diamonds, in right place. I want our M.P. to meet him,' he says.

MRS SCUFFHAM. Our M.P.

PARKER (*revelling in it*). That's what he said . . . It's my political future, you know: it's made. You'll be saying Councillor Parker soon. Then Alderman. *Then* what?

*The SOLDIER opens the window as before and thrusts his head in.*

SOLDIER.
    Then it'll be Doomsday. Hech!
(*He climbs in through the window.*)
    I'm climbing in for my breakfast.

> Doomsday's the day, mucker,
> Ye'll see wee maidens swift as lizards
> Running through the town,
> And all the polismen on the corners
> Give them brandy and red roses.
> Hech. That's the day for me, boy.

MRS SCUFFHAM (*appalled*). Did you say breakfast? Did you say breakfast?

SOLDIER. If ye havena got any, it doesna matter. Mr Scuffham, ye've given me twenty pounds already, I havena spent it, here it is – (*He shows the money in his breast-pocket.*) Am I no an honest soldier? But if ye wish to give me more, I think ye'd better let me have it now. Ye see, I've to leave this town. I can bide awa' from the regiment just so long – all right, it's detention. But longer than that, man, I'm for the glasshouse; and what service can I work for Johnny if I'm sharing his stone-cold cell? Tommy. Give me the money the day, I'll awa' off to Aldershot, so with the boys to Germany, then work it, work it, work it: he gets his retrial.

PARKER. Now, Serjeant, I've got a proposition . . .

SOLDIER. Och aye, the politics: ye telled me down the street. Plenty of time for that, now . . . But the money, I should have it this morning.

SCUFFHAM (*sulkily*). I'm not going to give you any money.

SOLDIER (*sharply*). What?

SCUFFHAM (*almost in tears*). I said I'm not going to give it you! I've been a man of chapel all my life, never touched a drop, never swore an oath . . .

MRS SCUFFHAM (*actually in tears*). The things I've done for that girl. All my cast-off dresses she's had, and there was that lovely blue hat with the cherries on: she turned up her nose . . .

SOLDIER (*understanding*).

> Och, is it *that* the gate the waters flow?
> She's of an age to know her mind,

And that's enough for all.
Tommy's Mary's Tommy's Mary:
But Tommy Scuffham's *yours.*

SCUFFHAM. You're getting nowt out of me, Mister Soldier.
You can go back to your murdering and your trampling on
sovereign rights of independent folk, and your shooting-
down of working men in the streets: but as far as this house
goes, you're done and you're capped. No two words.

PARKER (*anxiously*). Charlie, you're making a mistake there.
He's not that like of a soldier at all . . .

SOLDIER (*urgently*).
And no more is wee Tommy.
Will I tell ye, Mistress Scuffham,
What like of a soldier is *he*:
He's a scrub-neck convict in an Army jail,
With no more sovereign rights to *him*
Than are lost in the dust
Of a pew of your chapel!
Money? Or no money?
Does he have his retrial?

MRS SCUFFHAM. He's got to have that. He's our lad, Charlie
Scuffham. You've *got* to pay that money.

SCUFFHAM. I'm not paying owt.

MRS SCUFFHAM (*her voice rising*). You are!

SCUFFHAM. I'm not . . . I tell you I'm not . . . How much
does he want?

(*He refuses to look at the* SOLDIER.)

MRS SCUFFHAM (*very hard and hostile*). How much do you
want?

SOLDIER (*airily*). No more than ye can manage. Ye mentioned
forty-five quid . . .

MRS SCUFFHAM. That wor with my Post Office. I've not had
the time to draw it out.

SOLDIER. Then without your Post Office?

MRS SCUFFHAM. Thirteen over the twenty you've already got.

That's right, isn't it? . . . I said thirteen, Charlie Scuffham; is that right or isn't it?

SCUFFHAM (*reluctantly*). It's right.

MRS SCUFFHAM. Get it and give it him and let him go.

(SCUFFHAM *goes into the scullery.*)

(*To the* SOLDIER.) We're going to let you have that money because it's for our lad, but you're never to come here again. Not ever. You've done enough hurt to this house . . .

PARKER (*rather bewildered*). Now, Ida, be reasonable. I can't make out what you're getting at . . .

MRS SCUFFHAM. You mind your business, Nosey Parker; it's all your fault as it is . . .

PARKER. Here, I say, Ida . . .

MRS SCUFFHAM (*her voice rising very high*). You're the one as brought him here; you're the one as . . .

*The* SOLDIER *has been looking for something round the room.*

SOLDIER. Where's my tin whistle?

MRS SCUFFHAM (*startled in midstream*). Eh, what?

SOLDIER. My old tin whistle, Mistress. Left it on this table yesterday.

MRS SCUFFHAM. Well, it's not here now. And to speak true I don't care where it is. *I've* not laid a finger.

SOLDIER. *Someone's* laid a finger . . . *I* know what's happened to it . . .

*He starts for the stairs.*

MRS SCUFFHAM. Here, where are you going?

SCUFFHAM *comes in from the scullery with a dirty jam jar full of paper money. He, too, tries to intercept the* SOLDIER.

SCUFFHAM. Aye, where are you going? I'm not having you . . .

MRS SCUFFHAM. Not up there!

*But the* SOLDIER *is too nimble for them, and is already on the bottom steps. He holds them back with his hand.*

SOLDIER.

Wife, bairns, and rooftree
I may desert:
But my old tin whistle
Stays hooked to my heart.

(*He deftly twitches the handful of money out of* SCUFFHAM'S
*jam jar.*)

Down again in one half-minute.

*He goes up the stairs.*


MARY'S *bedroom.*

*She is crouching on the bed with her toy soldier. She has tears on
her face. The tin whistle has been laid carefully in front of the
madonna. She is running her belt through her fingers and pulling
at the knots in it. There are several more than before, and she
pulls them all to see that they are tight.*

MARY (*crooning*).

Come soldier, Come soldier,
Come soldier, *Come:*
The knots are tied tight
For to call you home.

(*The door is tried, but it is locked. There is a knock on it. Still
crooning.*)

Come soldier, Come soldier,
Come soldier, *Come:*
All the soldiers are dead soldiers
And you are alone.

*Another knock.*

THE SOLDIER'S VOICE. Mary, will ye open the door?

(*She gets up and opens the door. The* SOLDIER *comes in.
Business-like.*)

Where's my tin whistle?

MARY. I have not got it.

SOLDIER. Ach aye, ye've got it. Now, give it over here.

MARY (*as though stupidly*). I tell you I have not.

SOLDIER. It's in this room some place. Now where… Aha, so …

*He sees it and moves to get it.* MARY *holds him back.*

MARY. No.

SOLDIER. Na, na, na, lassie. That whistle's no for you.

MARY (*still holding him*). Nor for you now. It will stay where it's been given.

SOLDIER (*laughs roughly and sits down on bed*). Hech, this is rank robbery. Ye could be run into the clink.

MARY. Like Tommy.

SOLDIER. Aye, like Tommy. Now, let's have that whistle.

MARY. Or not like Tommy maybe? Do you know what I think? I think that Tommy was never in prison at all.

SOLDIER (*sharply*). Ye think that?

MARY. I think that.

SOLDIER (*looks at her shrewdly*).
>Aye? . . . Aye, well, now.
>Ye have a very pertinent notion there.
>Just as between two friends, now,
>What more *further* do ye think?

MARY (*very simply*).
>Or if he is in prison, you see:
>All that money you're asking,
>You'll keep it for yourself
>And not for him at all.
>That's what I think.

*The* SOLDIER *grins, very broad and slow, all the time looking at her. Suddenly he jumps to his feet and flings open the door.*

*The stairs.*

*The* SCUFFHAMS *and* PARKER *are in an undignified huddle*

*half-way up the stairs, trying to overhear the conversation, and are apparently moving upstairs by degrees.*

SOLDIER (*from off-screen*). Now, why don't yous three bide downstairs. Here's a *private* conversation takes place, awa' below with yous, hoot, hoot!

*They retreat, disappointed, into the living-kitchen.*

MARY'S *bedroom.*
*The* SOLDIER *comes in, and locks the door behind him. He has a confident, impudent smile on his face.*

SOLDIER (*satirically*).
    All right, lassie,
    So I'm just a randy chancer
    Hanging on your house
    And swindling your silver?
    You tell me that but I tell *you*
    There's green rushes on canal-side
    Wouldna dream those words was true,
    There's an old rotten barn roof
    At back of the glassworks wall
    Never heard *those* words
    Last evening or last night.
MARY (*dully*).
    Like rainfall or like snow they fall
    Words are black
    Or words are white.
SOLDIER.
    *Now* you'd say black:
    Last evening, naked white.
MARY (*looking up earnestly*).
    Then they were nothing at all

> You could call: words.
> Whistling and gone
> And leaves you trembling;
> Who knows what birds
> Then flapped across your grave?
> Among the rushes me and you
> I gave and you gave:
> *You* gave too.

SOLDIER (*sombre*). There's nothing left of that.

MARY. The green rushes whistle and preserve.

SOLDIER (*fierce and rough*).

> Preserve for who?
> The piles of rust and junk
> In Ellenroyd's yard?

(*He chants coarsely.*)

> Any old iron, any old iron,
> Here I'm a maid with a back to lie on
> Fetch me a soldier
> Before I'm much older
> For Tommy he's inside
> And my elbows raxing wide –
> All watery-golden
> Like a hoop of the sun . . .

(*He has allowed a certain softness to creep into the last two lines, so he roughens his voice consciously again.*)

But ye see it's done and ended, lassie. So let's have the old tin whistle.

MARY (*suddenly, after a pause*). How much of the money have they given you?

SOLDIER (*startled*). Hech?

MARY (*speaking very quickly*). I know that at least you've the twenty pounds. Have you more than that or what?

SOLDIER (*not catching her drift*). Is it the money?

MARY (*urgently*). But twenty's enough; it doesn't matter for the rest. You took that money because you told them lies, but I tell you no lies: I'm coming with you, soldier, and I'm living with you and that money's my only fortune and we're travelling today.

SOLDIER. Hey?

MARY. What do I care where we live? I've lived *here* two whole years, so Mother-of-God, what place is there I couldn't live . . .

SOLDIER. And what happens to Tommy?

MARY. I have no more life left for Tommy; all of my life is for you.

SOLDIER. Is that so . . .

MARY. I'm telling you no lies, boy.

SOLDIER (*furiously*). Nor I'm telling you none neither! God help us, a soldier's wife. D'ye imagine I've never met ye before, hell's devil eat your feet, woman – I *married* ye in Birmingham nineteen forty-one! I've tickled your pretty wee lugs and chuckled into your armpits in London and Fort George and Glasgow and Düsseldorf and Naples and Sidi Barrani, and ye're worse each time than the last, and it's this bloody time ye're the worst of bloody all.

(*She looks at him stupefied for a moment, and then starts to weep, or, rather, keen: a strange disconcerting moan which startles him considerably.*)

Ach awa' now, ye've no call for greeting: I'm telling ye truth and ye ken it well it's truth . . .

(*She continues to cry. He is nonplussed and irritated.*)

Mphm! And Irish this time, too.

Have they not always said it:

'An Irish wife
And an Irish knife:
Bright and white
And kill your life.'

Or would do, if ye're daft enough to let them. Well, I'll just get my whistle and awa' . . . God help us, will ye hold your noise!

MARY. You will not touch that whistle!

*She fiercely prevents him as he reaches for the whistle.*

SOLDIER (*trying to be reasonable*). Now, see here, lassie, what for d'ye have to go greeting and roaring like an old wife in a tram-smash. Ach, hearts-of-justice, did I not make it clear enough to ye the last day I was never a man for long companionings! I canna carry ye with me to the Army . . .

MARY. Why not?

SOLDIER (*despairing*). Why not . . .

MARY.

> Why go to the Army at all?
> Why not let's go to Ireland?
> What's the matter with Ireland?

SOLDIER. Ach, for the matter of that, what's the matter with Egypt, except it's full of Egyptians – or Irish, or whatever: or what the hell do *I* care!

> Look, I'm a travelling man now,
> But when I stop travelling, see:
> Here is the Army
> And it's a close house
> And there's square meals a day
> And it's a man's strong life
> Has four measured sides
> Like four forests round one farm
> And no foul weather except
> Is your own: or a war –
> And we'd be *all* of us in a *war* . . .

(*She has stopped weeping to hear him, but now she starts up again. He pulls money from his pocket.*)

Och, what's the use? I'd be talking till Christmas. Here, look, here's half of the twenty – look, look, I'll make it fifteen. *Now* will ye hold your greeting and let me gang in quiet!

MARY (*irrelevantly*). All these knots I tied for you. Pulling you round me so tight.

SOLDIER. All right, then, take the lot of it then – will ye take the whole flaming lot – take *thirty-three* quid and be damned!

*He throws the money across her bed.*

MARY (*strongly*). No, I will not! To be living with you, sure, I would take it, but to just steal the money from an old fool and his wife and to travel the world so with only stolen money and but one soul to hold it – no, I will not! Use it yourself, man; it's no good to me.

SOLDIER (*sourly*). No good to nobody – what's the bloody use . . .

(*He shovels up some of the money and stuffs it in his pocket, leaving the rest scattered. He turns to the door. With a sudden awkward tenderness.*)

Ye can keep the whistle, keep it: dance yourself a jig, whiles. Hech, ye're a bonny lassie: but I told ye that, last evening . . . Good-bye to ye so.

*He goes out, leaving her sobbing on the bed.*

*She is still lying on her bed, but no longer sobbing. She gets up slowly, pulls a shabby little suitcase from under the bed, opens it, and starts to pack it with clothes from her chest of drawers. She picks up her soldier and puts it in among the clothes, all anyhow. She takes up the belt, is about to pack it, then stands considering, and fingering the knots in it. With a sudden decision she ties it round her waist. She picks up the tin whistle, with a curious secret smile. She puts it to her lips, and after one or two false notes begins to blow a passable version of* 'Soldier, Soldier'.

*The living-kitchen.*

*The* SCUFFHAMS *and* PARKER *are clustered at the bottom of the stairs, listening. They hear the* SOLDIER'S *feet descending.*

MRS SCUFFHAM. He's coming down.

SCUFFHAM. Not afore time.

MRS SCUFFHAM. She wor crying and crying.

*They move away from the stairs as the* SOLDIER *comes into the room. He walks straight through the room to the front door, putting on his bonnet and picking up his swagger-stick as he passes.*

SOLDIER (*in a hectoring manner*). Is my breakfast ready? If not why not? Put it on the hob and I'll eat it when I'm back. *When* am I back? I canna tell ye . . .

*He goes out into the street.*

PARKER. Eh, Charlie, what *is* all this about?

MRS SCUFFHAM. What are we going to do, Charlie? However will we break it to our Tommy?

SCUFFHAM. Ah, you might well wonder: and no two words . . .

MARY *comes into the room, carrying her suitcase and wearing her outdoor clothes.*

MARY. Which way did he go?

SCUFFHAM. Which way . . .

PARKER. He went to the left.

MARY. He went to the railway station. Then I go to the right. That goes to the bus station.

MRS SCUFFHAM. But why to the bus . . .

MARY (*with a new, hard confidence*). So I can find my own road. I don't know where to. I don't care at all. Just out: and good-bye. You can tell my little husband, when he finally comes, that I used to love him once. I dare say he'll be glad for it.

*She goes out into the street.*
*There is a violent knocking on the front door.*

SCUFFHAM. *Now* what is it? Don't say he's forgotten summat . . .

*He opens the door and* MRS PARKER *hurries in.*

MRS PARKER. Is Joe Parker here?

PARKER (*surprised*). Hello, Alice.

MRS PARKER (*grimly*). Hello. I just met that soldier in street. Where's he off to?

(*They shrug their shoulders. She sits down.*)

Eh, let me get my breath . . . Hello, Ida. Was that Mary just went past?

MRS SCUFFHAM. That's right, Alice. I'm glad you've come when you did. We've a lot to tell you, Alice.

MRS PARKER. And I've a lot to tell *you*, and all! By, I've got some bright news for you!

PARKER. What sort of news?

MRS PARKER. Just a minute while I get my breath . . . So it's Joseph Smart Parker, is it, that chuffed-up about finding a soldier to yell 'Down with the Government', for him that he never thought on to ask a few plain questions first!

PARKER (*alarmed*). What are you talking about!

MRS PARKER. I'm talking about you. Eh, you can reckon you're fair lucky to have me at your back in your politics to stop you making yourself a complete public monkey. If ever you're elected, you can thank me first, I'm telling you . . .

MRS SCUFFHAM (*in fear*). Alice . . .

MRS PARKER (*triumphantly*). I said to myself this morning, I said, 'It's time I did some telephoning.' So I did some. And first lot I rang up was the War Office.

PARKER. The War Office!

MRS PARKER. The War Office. And what they told me . . .

*The pub. Lunch-time.*
*There are a fair number of customers, such as we have seen before, but a much more obvious air of conviviality. The hum of chatter is loud and we are not able to distinguish strands of conversation.*

*A good deal of business is being done at the bar. The tune 'Soldier, Soldier' is being whistled, and we discover that the performer is the* SOLDIER, *equipped with a new tin whistle and an admiring circle of drinkers. He finishes the tune with a flourish and there is some applause. He acknowledges this.*

SOLDIER. There's words to it, too. (*He sings.*)
> 'O Soldier, Soldier,
> Will ye marry me now,
> With a hey and a ho
> And a fife and drum?'

And then he tells her, ye see:
> 'O Lady, Lady,
> I canna marry you –
> Because I have
> No coat to put on.'

And so forth. Has every man a drink? All right, my boys, here's the boy that's paying – (*He addresses the* LANDLORD.) Snap it around mucker; they're all rioting for the drink.

*He throws money on the bar counter, and the drinkers cluster in with their orders.*

FIRST VOICE. Black-and-tan and a pint of bitter . . .
SECOND VOICE. I'll have a stout.
THIRD VOICE. Stingo for me, Billy . . .
FOURTH VOICE. Stingo and bitter . . .

*Etcetera.*
*The* LANDLORD *bustles about, serving them all. The* DRINKER *whom we have met before pushes away from the bar carrying a foaming glass, and sways across in front of the* SOLDIER, *nearly spilling his drink.*

DRINKER (*cheerfully*). Hey, soldier, did he marry the lass after all?

SOLDIER. Ha! He says to her, 'I havena got a coat,' he says. (*Sings*).

> 'So off she went
> To her grandfather's chest
> And she fetched him a coat
> Of the very very best
> Says: "Come on, me brave boy,
> Now put this on." '

(*He breaks off, staring at the door. We see that* PARKER *has just entered, and is looking at the* SOLDIER *in some astonishment.*)

Hech, it's Mr Parker!

What'll ye drink, Mr Parker?

Name it and it's served!

PARKER (*bitterly*). I didn't reckon to find *you* still here.

SOLDIER. Did ye no? Man, I've just bought myself a new tin whistle. I couldna leave this town without I'd tried it out.

PARKER. I think you and me, we'd better have a quiet word.

SOLDIER. Ach, aye, a quiet word. (*To those at the bar.*) I'm awa' to have a word.

*He and* PARKER *withdraw to a table in the far corner of the room, and sit down.*

PARKER. First I'd better tell you I've been making a few inquiries. This morning after breakfast I rang up the War Office.

SOLDIER (*airily*). Och, imagine.

PARKER (*righteously indignant*). You know what they told me? They told me as Tommy Scuffham warn't in prison at all.

SOLDIER. Then where is he?

PARKER. *They* don't know: *I* don't know. He was discharged medically unfit nine month since. That's the last as anyone's heard. But he's not in prison and he never has been in prison.

SOLDIER (*airily*). Och, imagine.

PARKER (*furiously*). Well then: what about it! You told me . . .

SOLDIER (*contemptuously*). I told ye this: I told ye that. Ye ask daft questions, ye got daft answers. Besides, I was three parts fou. I'll tell ye another thing. I never even heard of Johnny Scuffham before I met you that time.

PARKER. You never even heard . . .

SOLDIER. I'd to keep ye contented somehow. Och, man, d'ye imagine I ken every sock-headed man in the whole regiment?

PARKER (*spluttering*). Why – why – you know, I could get you ten year for this!

SOLDIER. Mphm. For what good that'll do ye . . . I'll tell ye what ye *will* do: ye'll gang up on your platform and ye'll tell your jolly muckers that your poor military victim's gone back to the Army – in manacles and leg-irons, if ye like. Ye might win your election. But tell them anything else, boy, and they'll laugh ye into the canal.

PARKER. What about Charlie Scuffham's money?

SOLDIER (*gesturing towards the crowd at the bar*). Hech, *what* about it? If he gangs and hires a stomach-pump, he'll maybe get his value. But for your own reputation, ye'd be advised to keep him quiet . . . And now you'll forgive me while I catch the afternoon train. If I dinna get to Aldershot the night, I'll be posted a deserter. And then I'd have to ask for forty pound so as to bribe ye for a false witness. (*He rises from the table and finishes his drink in a quick swallow.*) Good day to ye, mucker.

(*He walks toward the street door, calling to the crowd and the* LANDLORD *as he goes.* PARKER *is left sitting open-mouthed at the table.*)

Good day to the lot of yous. There's the money on the timber for drinks for every man.

*He walks out of the bar. The engraved glass door swings open and then shuts behind him.*

*The* SOLDIER *strides away from the pub, down the street,*

*towards the camera. We see him in long-shot at first.*

*Then a close-up of his boots swaggering along the pavement stones.*

*As he walks the drums and fifes come in with 'Soldier, Soldier' and we hear the* SOLDIER'S *voice singing the final verse of the song.* (*Sings.*)

'O Soldier, Soldier,
Will ye marry me now
With a hey and a ho
And a fife and drum.
O Lady, Lady,
How can I marry you
When I have already
A wife of my own?'

# Wet Fish

*A Professional Reminiscence for Television*

1960

WET FISH was first presented by BBC Television on 3 September 1961, with the following cast:

| | |
|---|---|
| RUTH PARSONS | Judith Stott |
| LESLIE | Anthony Valentine |
| PETER APPLEYARD | Edward Petherbridge |
| GILBERT GARNISH | Reginald Beckwith |
| TREDDLEHOYLE | Douglas Ives |
| SIGISMANFRED KRANKIEWICZ | Alan Edwards |
| DORIS TREDDLEHOYLE | Nancy Jackson |
| MRS HIGSON | Sheila Johnson |
| TEA-MAN | Arthur R. Webb |
| FRANK BARKER | Karl Bernard |
| PERKINS | Eric Jones |
| CUSTOMERS | { Peggy Hughes<br>Isobelle Swann |
| WORKMEN | { George Leyton<br>Geoffrey Tetlow<br>David Park<br>Michael Robbins |
| FOREMAN | Graham Rigby |
| ARCHDEACON POLE-HATCHET | Ralph Hallet |
| SIR HAROLD SWEETMAN | Arthur Pentelow |
| WAITER | Bill MacLaine |

Directed by Peter Dews

*The drawing-office of Gilbert Garnish and Partners.*

*A room on an upper floor with windows overlooking a main street. The walls are covered with architectural drawings, pinned up for reference: sexy calendars from contractors: picture postcards of celebrated contemporary buildings: shelves here and there littered with trade catalogues and professional journals.*

*There are four drawing-boards, each with an anglepoise lamp, arranged on long trestle tables, with drawers underneath for storage of plans.*

*The drawing-boards are seen by the camera one after the other in the following order.*

PETER'S *board – very neat, all his draughtsman's equipment tidy and carefully arranged to one side. His hand is seen ruling a precise line on a large-scale detail drawing.*

LESLIE'S *board. Not so neat. A picturesque pile of poster paints, etc., some copies of advanced architectural magazines. On his board is a newspaper spread out, and we see his hand at work on the crossword.*

KRANK'S *board. A working drawing spread out, covered with tracing-paper. Some miscellaneous documents strewn about, obviously relating to some contract. T-square, set-square, pencil. No personal objects at all. No occupant at the drawing-board either.*

RUTH'S *board. A chaos of papers, bits of drawing, paintboxes, pencils, etc. Her hand is seen working at a constructional drawing, ruling lines in ink. Her hair hangs over her T-square. We get the impression that she has made a kind of nest about her place of work and is thoroughly settled into it. While the camera picks up these details,* LESLIE *is heard whistling 'When father papered the parlour', loudly and out of tune.*

*A telephone, on a shelf against the wall in front of* LESLIE'S *drawing-board, starts to ring.*

RUTH'S *hand, holding her pen, jerks: and ink blotches her drawing.*

RUTH. Oh, bother the thing!

(*We now see her fully, in close-up. She is aged twenty-three, not particularly glamorous, but attractive in an earnest sort of way. She wears glasses, and a smock to protect her clothes. Her hair is supposed to be up: but most of it is down.*)

I say, isn't anyone going to answer the phone?

LESLIE *is aged twenty-five. Genuinely enthusiastic for his profession, but masking it with a conventional student boisterousness.*

LESLIE. It's only half past nine. Never take phone calls before tea-break. I've told you before.

(*He removes his newspaper to reveal a half-finished perspective of a pompous and unworthy office block, fourteen stories high.*)

Oh lord, this abortion! It makes me weep every time I draw another line.

RUTH. Well, but – Peter, the phone!

PETER *is a middle-aged young man of twenty-eight, precise, blunt and serious, not very intellectual.*

PETER. I'm busy.

RUTH. Oh . . . (*She gets up in irritation and goes to the telephone to answer it.*) Hello, Gilbert Garnish and Partners, architects: Chief Drawing-Office . . . Yes? . . . Oh, just a moment, I'll see . . . Peter, it's Mr Barker of Durable Construction Ltd.

PETER. Tell him I'll ring him back. (*Irritated.*) He'll have his drawings when they're done. Besides, *I've* got a word to say to Durable; but I prefer to say it in my own good time.

RUTH *goes back to the telephone.*

RUTH. Hello, Mr Barker. I've just spoken to the Senior Assistant – he says he can't talk at the moment, he's on the other line; yes, the other line; but he'll ring you back . . . What? . . .

(LESLIE *is hooking his T-square into the knot in the back of* RUTH'S *smock and deftly undoing it. She turns round furiously.*)
Oh! . . . What ? . . . Leslie! . . . Yes, Mr Barker, I'll tell him . . . Good-bye.

*She rings off hurriedly.*

LESLIE (*sings*).

A girl called Ruth lives up our town:
Watch her roll her stockings down
One two three below the knee
Oh my word what *did* we see . . .

(RUTH *advances at him with an uncorked bottle of ink, threatening.*)
Hey, hey, not the ink . . . no, God no, man, mind my perspective . . .

PETER. Watch it, he's coming!

RUTH *and* LESLIE *whip back into positions of industry as the door opens and* GARNISH *comes flying in.*
*He is a frenzied little round ball of energy, aged about forty-five: his voice betrays an original Yorkshire accent, now over-laid with an acquired refinement, but likely to break out again in its purity at moments of stress. When such moments occur, the pitch of his rapid speech leaps up into what is practically a shriek.*

GARNISH. Morning everybody. Come along, Jim, this way . . .

(*He is followed by* TREDDLEHOYLE, *a sober, rheumatic trades-man of between fifty and sixty, now wearing his best suit, somewhat awkwardly, and a little embarrassed to be in the office.*)
This is what we call the Chief Drawing-Office; not many in here, one, two, three, four, but they're all of 'em working on the special jobs I like to keep me own eye . . . one, two,

three, *four*? Who's missing? Where's that Polack? Hasn't he come in yet? *Late?*

PETER. Oh, he's come in all right, Mr Garnish; I expect he's down at the typing pool about his . . .

GARNISH (*sceptical*). Typing pool? *Is* he? He'd better be. Half past nine, look! I was in *my* office at eight-fifteen, let me tell you. Some of you young architects roll up to your work like you'd think you had shares in the bus company. Well: this is Mr Treddlehoyle. I like to call him my original client. I did my first job for him over twenty years ago: and he's come to see me today to do him another.

TREDDLEHOYLE (*shyly*). Good morning, gentlemen.

GARNISH. Mr Treddlehoyle: Peter Appleyard, my Senior Assistant.

PETER. Morning.

GARNISH. Peter's working on the – what is it? Yes, the new city bus terminal. All all right, Peter?

PETER. Yes, I think so. I've been having a bit of trouble with Durable Construction.

GARNISH. Any nonsense from those fellers, you tell Barker to come and see me. They're not a good firm, y'know. I won't use 'em again . . . Leslie, how's the pretty picture?

LESLIE. Oh, er – coming on all right, Mr Garnish.

GARNISH (*shows the perspective to* TREDDLEHOYLE). New office block for the Quicksnack Breakfast Food, subsidiary to Amalgamated Corn Products – you know, Sir Harold Sweetman – very big deal! Fourteen stories. Highest building in town . . . least it will be when it's up. There's a good half a million already into that . . .

TREDDLEHOYLE (*impressed*). Proper lush, eh? You're doing all right there, Gilbert.

GARNISH. Not bad, not bad . . . Hello, me old Ruthey! What are you on?

RUTH. I'm just helping Peter with his working drawings at the moment, Mr Garnish . . .

GARNISH. Are you? Any complaints, Peter? Happy in your work, dear? . . . Good, good! But I think we'll give you a change, all the same. I want you this morning to . . .

(KRANK *slides into the room. He is a curiously nondescript Pole, who must be nearly forty, but could be almost any age between twenty-five and fifty. He wears cheap round spectacles like army-issue ones and a shabby double-breasted suit. At the moment he also wears a macintosh and a shapeless felt hat and carries a mysterious holdall, which he deposits quickly under his table. He sits at his drawing board and starts some sort of work, all in the one movement.* GARNISH *is watching him sardonically.*)

Good morning!

KRANK. Good morning, Mr Garnish.

GARNISH. How's the typing pool?

(KRANK *blinks, bewildered.*)

My watch says five and twenty to ten.

KRANK. Yes, I know. So does mine, sir. Three and twenty to, to be exact.

GARNISH. Jim, this is Mr, er – we can't pronounce it anyway, so we call him Krank.

KRANK. Sigismanfred Krankiewicz, in fact. Good morning. (*He gives a formal little bow.*)

TREDDLEHOYLE. Good morning.

GARNISH. He just uses my office for his international telephone calls, that's all. Pay no attention . . . Come along, Jim. We'll settle down to business. I think you've seen everything . . . Altogether thirty-five assistants, five secretaries, three partners, and the engineers in the basement – not bad, is it? come along . . .

(*Still talking, he conducts* TREDDLEHOYLE *out. When he is outside the door and the office is relaxing he suddenly calls back in again.*)

Ruth! You come, too! I'm going to give you some work.

RUTH (*in a flurry*). Oh! Yes, Mr Garnish. Shall I bring my . . .

PETER. Go on, love, don't keep him waiting.

*She gathers up a notebook and pencil and hastens out after.*
*LESLIE sends a whistle at her as she goes.*

LESLIE. Run, rabbit, run!

*Garnish's private office.*
*A considerable contrast to the preceding room. Very luxurious and tastefully designed, large desk, expensive drawing-table with virgin drawing-paper on the board, framed perspectives and photographs of the firm's designs on the walls, daring light fittings, battery of telephones on the desk, elegant architect-designed chairs.*
GARNISH *comes in with* TREDDLEHOYLE, *and* RUTH *following.*

GARNISH. Right, here we are, Jim, sit down, sit down, sit down. Cigar?

*He hands him an elaborately simple silver cigar box on the desk.*

TREDDLEHOYLE. Why, I don't mind if I – perhaps I'd better not; I'm not really supposed . . . oh well, what's the odds? Thank you very much.

*He accepts the cigar.*
GARNISH *takes one too, and lights both with an elaborately simple silver lighter from his desk.*

GARNISH. Well, what d'you think of it?

TREDDLEHOYLE. Eh, you've done yourself proud. I can tell you that without forswearing, Gilbert. Like, I'm a bit over-come.

GARNISH. Oh no, surely not? How d'you mean?

TREDDLEHOYLE. Why, it's a long haul back to 1938. You hadn't even an office in them days, had you?

(RUTH *meanwhile is hanging about awkwardly, waiting for instructions.* GARNISH *glances at her now and then to observe the effect of these flattering reminiscences.*)

I'll tell you this, Gilbert: it wor a first class fish-shop. It put the business up like *that!* Why, me old dad said to me, 'We're like *floating* in fish: fish up to the knees, and money to the elbows.' O'course, though, he's dead now.

GARNISH. Is he?

TREDDLEHOYLE. Oh aye, ah, in forty-five he went under. It wor the end of the war did for him really. V-day and that, you know. We wor open two nights running, all night, *thousands* of customers, all in the pouring rain, bellowing for chips. Well, the steam, and the condensation, it finished him off. Went straight to his back. Bent him up like a whiting . . . Eh, dear . . . Now, you see, I've got the same trouble. I want you to cure it.

GARNISH (*jocular with some embarrassment*). I can give a massage any day you want, lad . . . click, click, click-click, eh? (*He rubs his hands together in a parody of a masseur, and laughs.*)

Joking apart, though: I know what you're after. It's the open-fronted shop, isn't it? You want it closed in. Shouldn't be too difficult. Now I've taken the trouble to have out the old plans.

(*He opens a drawer in a plan chest and whips out a rather dog-eared drawing.*)

Ruth, come here . . . Miss Parsons is going to be working with me on this.

(*He spreads the plan out on his drawing-board and they group themselves around it to have a look.*)

Now, you see what we want, Ruth: the wet-fish department had an open front in the old style, clear out to the street. Now, we can put in a big window, here, closing it all in; I should think a glazed door in this corner; move the counter back three foot, three foot six, no, make it four feet and call ourselves generous . . . then we can . . .

TREDDLEHOYLE. Eh, wait on, wait on, don't go so fast. I've not said it all yet. You see, my good lady's got views about this. She said to me at first, 'With your rheumatism getting like it is, I'm not having you working in that open shop any more.' The doctor's forbidden it, and all. So her idea was, she should take over the wet fish and leave me alone wi' the chip counter inside, where I could bide in the warm. But I wouldn't have it. I said no: wet fish for me wor the start o' my business, and it's going to be the end. Fish and chips is a side-line, whatever my dad did. So we'll put both departments in one and we'll close 'em all in. Now, that's going to involve . . .

GARNISH. Ruth, are you watching? You're going to have to *do* this, you know!

RUTH. Yes, Mr Garnish.

GARNISH. This affects the position of your W.C., doesn't it?

TREDDLEHOYLE. Does it? . . . Oh aye, so it does . . . How much do you reckon it's all going to cost?

GARNISH. Cost? . . . H'm . . . Three thousand?

TREDDLEHOYLE (*taken aback*). Three thousand . . .

GARNISH. That's an outside estimate, of course. We may find we can cut it down quite a bit once we get going, but . . . (*His telephone rings. He goes to answer it.*) Excuse me a minute . . . Yes, Garnish here . . . What? . . . Look, it's not a bit of use my meeting the Archdeacon without Sir Harold being there as well; it's just duplicating conferences and a waste of time for everybody . . . Hang on a moment, please . . .

(*He presses the buzzer of his office intercom and speaks into another mouthpiece.*)

Miss Waters? Will you check on the correspondence we had last week with Sir Harold Sweetman; there was a letter saying when he was going to be available for . . . Right, right, well hurry it up then; I've got the Cathedral on the blower . . . Right.

(*He holds both receivers against his body and speaks to* TREDDLEHOYLE.)

The Lady Chapel's falling down.

(*The voice from the Cathedral speaks again and he listens.*)

What . . . what's that? Next week? . . . All right then, suits me. Good-bye.

(*He rings off that line and speaks to his secretary once more.*)

Miss Waters? No panic after all, dear. Not to worry.

(*He rings off and heaves a sigh of relief.*)

Well, I think that's about the lot, isn't it, Jim? All you need to do now is leave it with us. I'll get you out a drawing, Miss Parsons will send it for you to see, we'll get on to the quantity surveyors and put it out for tenders. All right?

TREDDLEHOYLE. Right, Gilbert, that's fine . . . You know, three thousand pound's a bit more than I wor bargaining for.

GARNISH. Don't you worry, boy: we'll look after you.

TREDDLEHOYLE. . . . I – I put a lot of faith in you, Gilbert. You did very well by us before . . . Right, well, I'll save this for after me dinner. Good morning . . .

*He puts his cigar remainder carefully away, fumbles with his hat and moves towards the door.*

GARNISH *buzzes again and speaks to his secretary.*

GARNISH. Miss Waters! (*He opens the door for* TREDDLE-HOYLE.) 'Bye, Jim.

TREDDLEHOYLE. Good-bye.

TREDDLEHOYLE *goes out.* GARNISH *dodges back to the intercom.*

GARNISH. And Miss Waters, get me Mr Perkins of Price and Perkins, will you?

(*He rings off and turns to* RUTH.)

Now then, Ruth; how long have you been with us?

RUTH. Just about a year, Mr Garnish.

GARNISH. You came just after you qualified, didn't you? What jobs have we had you working on? H'm? A bit of

everything, in fact? Right? Well, for a change, I'm going
to give you a job all on your own. Here it is. It's not difficult.
You've heard what Mr Treddlehoyle wants. Can you do it?

RUTH. Oh yes, I expect so; I'm sure I can, Mr Garnish . . .

GARNISH. Good!

(*The telephone rings. He answers.*)

Hello: Garnish! . . . Right . . . (*He speaks to* RUTH.)
This is Price and Perkins, I want them to be the quantity
surveyors on this job: now you make sure they have all the
drawings they need – Hello, Mr Perkins? . . . And how
are *you*, sir? . . . Ha, ha, well: you'll get your opportunity,
because we're rebuilding a chip shop and I'd like you to take
the quantities, if you will . . . Send one of your young
men round; he can talk to our Miss Parsons . . . Right:
good: thank *you*, Charlie: good-bye. (*He rings off.*) Now
let's have the drawings as quick as possible, Ruth, because
I mean to see this job done well.

RUTH. Yes, Mr Garnish.

GARNISH. Any problems that occur to you?

RUTH (*at the drawing*). No . . . no . . . I was thinking, if
we've to knock this wall out, it'll mean a girder supported
by a pier, here – at least, it seems to me – I mean, it doesn't
leave much room for the glass door you were talking about
. . .

GARNISH. Doesn't it? Ah . . . no more it does, either, Miss
Sharpeyes, eh? That's what I pay you young architects for,
y'know. I provide the jobs and you do 'em: otherwise *none*
of us'd get breakfast. Would we? Ha ha. All right then: do
your best.

(*The telephone rings. He answers.*)

Hello: Garnish! . . . Yes . . . Good morning to *you*, sir
. . . All right, Ruth: off you go!

(*She goes with drawing and he devotes himself to his caller.*)

Now I'm very glad you rang. I'd been wanting to have a
word for some days about your chimneys.

*Treddlehoyle's shop: the office.*
*This is a very small room that opens out of the wet-fish department.*
*A pigeon-hole desk stuffed with bills, receipts, invoices, etc. A*
*calendar or two from trade associates, a picture of the Queen and*
*another of Sir Winston, some comic picture postcards and some*
*with views of seaside places – all pinned up on the wall without*
*much conscious arrangement. A tiny window looks out into a*
*backyard.* DORIS *is sitting at the desk looking through ledgers*
*and comparing bills. She is a handsome blonde in her early*
*thirties, something of the barmaid about her. She wears an overall,*
*for serving in the shop.*

DORIS (*singing to herself*).
     'When father papered the parlour
     You couldn't see him for paste:
     Dabbing it here, dabbing it there,
     Dabbing it just about everywhere . . .'
  (*She breaks off to shout through the half-open door.*)
  You can afford it!
TREDDLEHOYLE (*from outside*). I can't and I won't, that's
  flat.
DORIS (*without taking her attention away from her accounts*).
  You can! You could pay out *four* thousand and we'd still
  have enough to buy a new mat for the bathroom. What
  about that two hundred?

*Treddlehoyle's shop: the wet-fish department.*
*An open-fronted style fish shop, quite smart and modern (it was*
*built in 1938), with a central fish slab. A door opens into the*
*frying department (which is also entered from the street) – at the*
*back is a little lobby with three doors in it; one of them leads into*
*the office, another on to the staircase, the third into the lavatory.*

*There are at present no customers.* TREDDLEHOYLE, *wearing an overall and a striped apron, is washing down his slab and arranging the display of fish. His wife's voice continues calling to him from the office.*

DORIS. I say what about that two hundred you lent to Joe Parker when he wor thinking of standing for the Council? He ought to be paying it back.

TREDDLEHOYLE (*sourly*). Back? Time he pays it back there won't be a fish shop at all, just four open walls wi' the seaweed creeping up. I can't afford three thousand quid! Oi-oi-, here's a customer coming . . .

(*An elderly miserable woman,* MRS HIGSON, *wanders into the shop.*)

How are you, Mrs Higson?

MRS HIGSON. Poorly. What's the cod like this morning?

TREDDLEHOYLE. Cod? It'd do to mend a pair o' boots, that's about all. Herrings is nice, though.

MRS HIGSON. I'm not over-set on a pair of herrings, today. They're like to come a bit greasy, aren't they? Mr Higson's sometimes fond of a kipper . . .

DORIS (*in the office*). You can afford it!

TREDDLEHOYLE (*exasperated*). I can't and I – Just a minute, Mrs H., I'll be back . . .

*He goes over to the door of the office.*


*Treddlehoyle's shop: the office.*
TREDDLEHOYLE *sticks his head in, angrily.*

TREDDLEHOYLE. Just shut up about money while I've got rid of Mrs Higson. I don't want all Intake Road to know my bank balance!

DORIS. Four thousand five hundred'd be none too much, I'm telling you.

TREDDLEHOYLE. Now just you shut up!

*Treddlehoyle's fish shop: the wet-fish department.*
TREDDLEHOYLE *slams the office door and returns to his customer.*

TREDDLEHOYLE. Sorry Mrs H., matrimonial ructions. Are you having the kippers then?
MRS HIGSON. I think so: if they're not over-bony. I'll take a couple o'pair . . . Mrs Treddlehoyle said you wor thinking o' flitting?
TREDDLEHOYLE (*weighing and wrapping the kippers*). Flitting? We may be reconditioning. I dunno which is the worst.
MRS HIGSON. Going all contemporary, eh?
TREDDLEHOYLE (*alarmed*). Eh? I hope not! Two and a penny: all right? It's just I'm getting a bit old for the wet floors and that. Have you got the odd penny?
MRS HIGSON (*who has presented a note*). Aye, I think so . . . Will you be having to close, then?
TREDDLEHOYLE. 'Business as usual during alterations', but it's bound to muck us up a bit. Eh dear, I don't know . . .
MRS HIGSON. We'll look forward to seeing it: when it transpires. Good morning.
TREDDLEHOYLE. Good morning, Mrs Higson.

*As* MRS HIGSON *goes,* DORIS *comes through into the shop.*

DORIS. You'd better make your mind up, sharp. Either you pay out what you can afford and get a new dry shop: or *I* pay out considerable less, and you get your coffin.
TREDDLEHOYLE. Gilbert Garnish is a fine lad, he's done very well for himself. And after all, y'know: it wor me that put him on the road.
DORIS. Well then.
TREDDLEHOYLE. Well, I don't know . . . I just hope he's

not wanting to turn this place into an addendum to the Ritz-Carlton Palace – I just hope he's not going to – oh – (*He gives way to his inner troubles.*) I don't *want* a new shop! I'm very fond of me old one! *I* didn't ask to get all these rheumatics in me back – why, I could last out another twenty year! I shall cancel the whole damn thing!

DORIS. You won't.

TREDDLEHOYLE (*subsiding*). Oh . . . Here, have those lobsters arrived from Whitby yet?

DORIS. No, they haven't.

TREDDLEHOYLE. Will you ring 'em up, and ask 'em why not! I don't seem to be able to get any reliability out of anybody these days. I don't know what's the matter . . .

*Garnish's drawing-office.*
*All four assistants are busy at work.* RUTH *is painting a perspective interior of her fish-shop design. It is an attractive scheme – she can obviously present her architectural ideas with some facility. She stands back from her drawing-board with her paintbrush poised.*

RUTH (*to the office at large*). Maroon. I'm not very fond of maroon. Who thinks blue?

LESLIE (*crooning over his drawing-board in an abstracted way*). 'Blue skies, everywhere blue skies, Smiling at me . . .' I make it tea-time.

RUTH. Oh, bother it! Blue! Krank?

KRANK (*looking up from his work*). What is to be blue?

RUTH. Mr Treddlehoyle's tiles.

KRANK. Floortiles, rooftiles, walltiles?

RUTH. Walltiles.

KRANK. No.

RUTH. Why not? I like it.

LESLIE (*lewdly*). *I* like it, too.

PETER. We all know what *you* like.

RUTH. But it's fish.

KRANK. Fish, yes, very cold. Good. But around it – warm, generous, old gold, vermilion.

RUTH. He'd never pay for all that. Peter, what do you think?

*PETER comes over to her drawing-board.*

PETER. Let's have a dekko. There's a good range of coloured tiles put out by Clayform Ltd. You want to look at their catalogue . . . Is that all the space you're leaving at the corner of the counter?

RUTH. It's enough, isn't it? Four foot six?

PETER. Well, if you think so. Your job, not mine.

*He moves away and goes to the telephone.*

LESLIE (*with sudden violence*). Tea! What's happened to the tea in this barrack! It's time Gibby Garnish sorted out his ancillary services. Tea tea tea, I want my tea!

*He beats on his drawing-board. PETER is talking on the telephone.*

PETER. Will you get Mr Barker of Durable Construction, please?

*KRANK also comes to the telephone.*

KRANK. I have a call booked. Excuse me.

PETER (*crossly*). You would. Wouldn't you?

*He moves away. KRANK takes the receiver and talks into it.*

KRANK. Hello, have you got me that number yet, please? 27869. Thank you . . .

*He holds on.*

RUTH. I should have thought four foot six was quite enough. Leslie, what do you think? Look . . . Oh, go on, Peter: even his widest customer couldn't be *this* size.

LESLIE. You'd be surprised what they can run to, up the Intake Road.

KRANK (*on telephone*). Hallo-allo! Can I speak to Mr Gromek, please? . . . Yes, yes . . . Ah, Stanislaw! Krankiewicz . . .

*He rattles away in urgent Polish.*

PETER (*looking at him in disgust*). Eh dear. Jabber jabber jabber. Twenty minutes wait.

GARNISH *comes in.*

GARNISH. Afternoon all.

ALL (*except* KRANK). Good afternoon, Mr Garnish.

GARNISH. How are we doing? Afternoon, Krank!

(KRANK, *still talking, waves his fingers in an airy salute, and continues his conversation.* GARNISH *comes to* RUTH'S *drawing-board.*)

Ah, that's a bit of all right, isn't it? Blue? Don't like it. Look better in green, but you're the architect. Carry on. And . . . er . . . leave enough room for his customers, won't you? Seems a bit cramped to me . . .

(*He moves round the room, looking at the others' work.*)

Good, good, all doing well . . . As soon as you've got that finished, Ruth, send it off to Mr Treddlehoyle. Right. Good. Keep him busy.

KRANK *finishes his telephone conversation and rings off.* PETER *immediately takes his place at the instrument.* KRANK *intercepts* GARNISH *as the latter is going towards the door.*

KRANK (*whispers*). Mr Garnish: excuse a moment, please.

GARNISH. Hello there, finished with the Kremlin

PETER (*simultaneously on phone*). Hello, can I speak to Mr Barker, please? . . . Mr Barker, Appleyard of Garnish and Partners here.

for this afternoon? What can I do for you?

KRANK. It's a question of a little matter of some property.

GARNISH. If you want me to stand security, lad, on one of your speculations in dosshouses, you'd better do your best to convince me it's legal. See me at five-thirty. I'm not promising anything. And to justify my trust in your integrity, why not do a bit of work for me for a change?

I was wondering if you had received my Variation Order No. 17 for the bus station; we've had no acknowledgement ... I would like to point out that if you had notified us in the first place that the specified pattern of sliding shutters were *not* available, we could have changed the design long ago, and there'd be no need at all for a variation *now*. Good afternoon. (*He rings off.*)

GARNISH *turns abruptly away from* KRANK, *has his hand on the door-handle to go out, gives his parting farewell to the office.*

Afternoon, everybody, carry on with the . . .
(*He opens the door with a flourish and walks straight into the* TEA-MAN, *a decrepit old skiver in a soiled overall coat, who is on the threshold, poising a tray loaded with teapot, milk-jug and cups, preparatory to coming in.*)
What's all this? *Tea!* How many times a day do I give you lot tea in these offices? Eight? When the Japanese rule the world, you can thank my grocery bill!

GARNISH *goes.*
*The* TEA-MAN *totters in, and deposits his load on a table. The assistants immediately crowd round.*

TEA-MAN. Now take it easy, take it easy, you'll have it all over the floor . . .

*He disengages himself from the jostling, and goes out.*

*Treddlehoyle's fish-shop: the frying department. A bright, bare room, with white walls and metal-topped counter.*
DORIS *is polishing the frying equipment and arranging fish and potatoes, etc., ready for work.*
TREDDLEHOYLE *has* RUTH'S *drawings (completed) spread out on the counter and is studying them, together with the accompanying letter.*

TREDDLEHOYLE. I think it's very good. I think it's very good indeed. I like it. Green walls, red floor, patent non-slip tiles, you see . . .
(*He beckons his wife over to look, too.*)
Contiguous frying department, and he's shifted the toilet. What did I tell you? He's a good man, is young Garnish. No damn nonsense at all.

DORIS. What happens next, then?

TREDDLEHOYLE. Get it out to contract, love. Two thousand five hundred, he says here. A very reasonable advance estimate. You see, he's brought it down. I hope he can find a builder to bring it down further. I told you, he's a good man. We're doing the right thing.

DORIS. I hope it won't be skimped.

TREDDLEHOYLE. Ah no, it won't . . . Well, I feel right chuffed-up about this. I think we'll have a bottle of stout to us suppers tonight. What do you say?

DORIS (*enthusiastically*). All right!

TREDDLEHOYLE. All *right*. I'll go and get one. Ho-ho, yes, I like it . . .

*He picks up a small blackboard chalked 'Frying tonight at six', sets it in the window, claps on his hat, and goes out into the street.*

*Garnish's private office.*
GARNISH *is talking on the telephone.*

GARNISH. Hello, is that Durable Construction, Ltd? . . .
Good. Mr Barker there? . . . Gilbert Garnish speaking
. . . Ah, Mr Barker. Have you finished that bus station for
us yet? . . . What? Not? Now look here, Mr Barker, those
precast columns ought to have been on the site three weeks
ago. It's not good enough, you know. Is it? However . . .
*however*, Mr Barker, I've got some more agreeable informa-
tion for you. I've just been comparing the tenders for the
fish-shop alterations in Intake Road. Yours is much the
lowest and so is your estimated completion date. So I have
great pleasure, sir, in offering you the contract!

*Barker's office.*
*All we see of this room is a cluttered desk with its telephone, and
the wall behind with charts of work-in-progress, and the usual
calendar (from a firm of engineers, with a large picture of steel
framework being built).*
BARKER *is at his telephone. He is shifty-looking, jolly-good-fellow
sort of fellow, with a brisk moustache.*

BARKER (*servilely into the telephone*). That is extremely
gratifying, Mr Garnish! May I say, sir, we will put forth
our very very utmost to expedite the job and that it is with
the greatest satisfaction that we receive your instructions
. . . Thank *you*, Mr Garnish. And as regards the bus-
terminal columns, I am making it my personal concern to
finalize every undertaking. They *will* be on the site this week,
I give you my word . . . Thank *you*, sir, good morning.

*He rings off and rubs his hands with satisfaction.*

*Garnish's office.*
GARNISH *rings off as well.*
*We now see that* RUTH *has been standing behind his desk during the telephone conversation.*

GARNISH. Ye-es . . . Well, Ruth, there we are. Now, they've no excuse whatever for falling down on a little job like this. Besides Barker's brother is going to be chairman of the reconstituted City Housing Committee next month, and the sooner you young architects learn the importance of bearing *that* sort of detail in mind, the sooner you'll get on in the profession.

RUTH. But they did send in the lowest tender?

GARNISH (*emphatically*). Of course they did, girly. I couldn't appoint them if they hadn't . . . it'd be cheating Mr Treddlehoyle. And in this business, you never ever try to pull a fast one over your client. Morality. Right? But a great deal depends upon which firms you ask to tender in the first place . . . All good experience, store it away . . . Right. Well, the next thing is a site meeting. We want Treddlehoyle, Barker, Perkins and, of course, ourselves. Friday a good day? (*He consults his desk diary.*)
All right, Friday. Miss Waters'll fix it up. Bring a tape-measure.

*Treddlehoyle's fish shop: the wet-fish department. It being Friday, the shop is busy.*
DORIS *is serving customers.*
RUTH *is climbing a step-ladder, taking measurements at the top of the doorway leading to the office.*

RUTH. Two foot six, no . . . no seven. If we drop the ceiling one foot, then we'll still have seven inches clearance above the top of the lintels. Mr Garnish, seven inches clearance . . . Mr Garnish!

GARNISH, TREDDLEHOYLE, BARKER *and* PERKINS, *a precise, lawyer-like little man in a bowler hat, are standing at the entry of the shop, in a huddle round some drawings.* GARNISH *looks back towards* RUTH.

GARNISH. Eh, what? Oh. Should be enough, shouldn't it? Good. Well, that's the last of the points I wanted to clear up. Any problems for you, Mr Perkins?

PERKINS. No. I think we've got about everything fixed.

GARNISH. What about Mr Barker? He's looking wise and saying nowt. What's on your mind, Frank?

BARKER *has put on a pair of horn-rims to look at the drawing. Now he takes them off and fiddles with them.*

BARKER. Access to the site. I've got a cement-mixer to put somewhere, but if Mr Treddlehoyle wants to keep a space clear for serving customers . . . What about the alleyway outside? Who does that belong to? Mr Treddlehoyle?

TREDDLEHOYLE *has drifted away towards his busy wife.*

GARNISH. Jim! The alleyway, whose is it?

TREDDLEHOYLE. Oh, that's just the little ginnel leads through into my yard. You can stick your machinery there all right. It won't be in anybody's road.

(*He takes money from a customer.*)

Thank you, Mrs Baxter, and I'll send you up the haddock on Tuesday. Good morning.

(*He returns towards them.*)

Everything done, gentlemen?

GARNISH. Yes, that's the lot. Mr Barker reckons he can start work on the twenty-seventh . . .

BARKER (*facetiously*). The Republic of Ireland permitting. I

mean, our labour force, Mr Treddlehoyle, you understand?
God help us!

GARNISH. O.K. with you?

TREDDLEHOYLE. Oh aye, we'll be ready . . . Don't be off
just yet a while, gentlemen. I've got a little summat in the
back office I'd like you to have a sample at, if you feel you
can spare the time. Straight through this way. I'll be with
you directly . . .

(*He ushers them across the shop towards his office, and calls to*
DORIS.)

Doris!

DORIS. Hello?

*He pushes through to her and starts a whispered conversation.
The men go on into the office, except* GARNISH, *who intercepts*
RUTH *as she comes down the ladder.*

GARNISH. While we're on the site, girly, it might be a good
idea if you checked your floor areas . . . I told you your
drawing looked a bit cramped, so why don't you dodge
around this counter for a few minutes and see how much
room you really *do* need? All right?

RUTH. Right, Mr Garnish.

TREDDLEHOYLE (*to* DORIS, *as he moves away from her*). When
you've got this lot served, come on in and join us . . . like,
we want to launch the boat proper, don't we?

DORIS. We do. I'll be with you.

TREDDLEHOYLE (*takes* GARNISH *by the arm*). Come on,
Gilbert, come on, what are we waiting for? There's a cork
to be pulled out, and I know the lad with a right elbow for
it eh? . . .

*He leads him into the office.*


*Treddlehoyle's fish shop: the office.*
TREDDLEHOYLE *comes in with* GARNISH.

*The other two are already there, and the little room is full.*

TREDDLEHOYLE (*taking a bottle of whisky from a compartment of the desk, and glasses*). You don't mind giving it a turn, do you, Gilbert? My wrists aren't all they ought to be these days; it's about all I can do to gut a herring, eh dear . . .
(GARNISH *opens the bottle.*)
Many thanks . . .
(*He pours out the drinks.*)
This is a bit be way of a celebration-in-advance, I know, but . . .
(*He drinks a toast.*)
Best o' good luck with the job, eh?

BARKER. Cheers.

PERKINS. I trust all goes well.

GARNISH. And here's to your rheumatism, Jim. It's rapid removal . . . Best damp-course you could want here. I don't know why we don't specify it as a matter of rule on all o' these jobs.

BARKER. One part water-repellent cement to two parts sand together with three parts proved Scotch whisky, trowelled smooth with a fair splayed edge . . . how about that in a Bill of Quantities, eh, Mr Perkins?

PERKINS. Ha ha, yes. I imagine it would need plenty of careful testing before it was passed fit for use. Oh yes, ha ha, testing most important . . . yes, well, I will have another, thank you very much, Mr Treddlehoyle. Very pleasant indeed.

TREDDLEHOYLE. Ha ha, y'know, excuse me, I've just got it: you mean, you trowel the Scotch up the wall to keep out the water . . . eh . . . that's not bad, is it? Ha ha, have another, Gilbert? Not bad, eh? By, you have to laugh . . . Mr Barker? . . .

*Treddlehoyle's fish shop: the wet-fish department.*

DORIS *serving customers as before.*

*What we see is* RUTH *on her knees among a forest of legs and shopping-baskets, measuring the floor.*

*The shoppers' dialogue goes on above her, while she mutters about her work to herself.*

RUTH. Three foot nine. Then eight and a half here . . . Oh, bother it . . . excuse me, if I could reach past your knee, just this way, excuse me . . . four foot six, four foot six ? . . . Oh, easy four foot six, this is only four foot two . . . Who says it's going to be cramped ? You could do it in under four foot . . . Four foot ?

FIRST CUSTOMER. Pound of fillet cod, please, Doris, and have you got any herring roes ?

DORIS. We're out of roes, I'm afraid. We're all in a jumble today. We've got the builders in.

FIRST CUSTOMER. Cups o' tea, that's what they'll want. You'll be brewing up all day.

DORIS. The sooner they're in, the sooner they'll be out, two-and-six, thank you, who's next ?

*As she says* 'Four foot', RUTH *looks up through the space she has been measuring to see an enormously fat woman standing in front of her.*

Well, four foot eight *might* be safer . . . Excuse me . . .

FAT WOMAN (*jovially*). Are you taking a measure of *me*, love ?

RUTH. Well, no, not exactly . . .

FAT WOMAN. Eh, you'll need a longer tape nor you've got there. Are you fitting us all up wi' new corsets while you're at it, Doris ? It'll be a few years afore you can reach my size, love. I remember when they wor doing us all out for corsets at the Infirmary, time the National Health come in . . . eh, by, that wor a sight ! There wor a young doctor there, he says 'Move along the elephants,' he says. 'Circus just about to begin,' he says. Eh by, heh heh heh, you had to laugh, 'Move along the elephants,' he says – heheh heh, you had to . . .

*GARNISH appears at the office door.*

GARNISH. Ruth?
RUTH. Er, yes . . .
GARNISH. Have you done yet? Come on in, come on!
RUTH. Yes, Mr Garnish.

*She gets up and goes into the office with him.*

*Treddlehoyle's fish shop: the office.*
*Conviviality is well under way as GARNISH comes in with RUTH.*
*They are all laughing at something BARKER has just been saying.*

BARKER. It's no good, it's no damn good at all, y'know; the Labour Party won't hear of it. And it'd bring more money into the city than thirty-three new bus stations . . . Here, Gilbert, I've just been telling Charlie Perkins about that Prince Consort Street project; the more I think about it, the more I see . . .

GARNISH. I'll have a word with you about that later, Frank, if you don't mind . . . Jim, this little lady's been outside among the fillet-soles for the last twenty minutes and she needs a bit of waterproofing, same as the rest of us. Right?

TREDDLEHOYLE. *That's* the word to give me; here you are then – whoops, sorry, cheers.

*He fills RUTH a glass with some inaccuracy.*

BARKER. Cheers!
PERKINS. It's politics, always politics; they turn everything that's brought-up into a confounded party-issue! It's as

bad as it was in the Army . . . Well, I really must be on
my way, Mr Treddlehoyle; thank you very much indeed
. . .

TREDDLEHOYLE (*detaining him*). Eh dear no, not yet, Mr er
. . . go on, swallow it down!

*He forces* PERKINS *to have another.*

BARKER (*to* GARNISH). D'you remember old Toby Theak-
stone? Full Colonel he would have been, by the end of the
war . . . he had No. 9 Bridging Group at one time.

TREDDLEHOYLE. I got my war wound in forty-four. Twenty-
two kilometres south of Rome . . . five damn great Stukas
come over . . . whrrr, boom!

*He gives a graphic imitation of dive-bombing, which goes
generally unregarded.*

PERKINS (*rather excited*). *I* knew him, *I* knew Toby Theak-
stone. I ran his Costings Office for him before he transferred
to Airfields Construction. He used to . . .

BARKER. Good old Toby, eh? He was a credit to the Corps!

*He breaks into song (The Royal Engineers March):* GARNISH
*joins in and then* PERKINS. *All three complete the song with
great enthusiasm:*

'Good morning, Mr Steven
And a windy, notchy night
Hurrah for the CRE!
We are working very hard
Down at Upnor Hard
Hurrah for the CRE!
You make fast,
I make fast,
Make fast the dinghy,
Make fast the dinghy,
Make fast the dinghy.

You make fast,
I make fast,
Make fast the dinghy,
Make fast the dinghy, Pontone.
For we are marching on to Laffan's plain,
To Laffan's plain,
To Laffan's plain,
Yes, we are marching on to Laffan's plain
Where they don't know mud from clay.
Ah ah ah ah ah ah ah ah.
Ooshta ooshta ooshta ooshta.
Ikona malee picaninny skoff
Maninga sabenza, here's another oss.
"Oolunda," cried Matabele,
"Oolunda, away we go!"
Ah ah ah ah ah ah ah.
Shwsh . . . Hurrah!'*

DORIS *has come into the office.*
*She reaches the bottle from her husband's hand and pours herself a drink.*
*She finds herself next to* RUTH, *who is squashed up into a corner.*

DORIS. Building-trade exerting every effort, eh?
(BARKER, *while singing, sees* DORIS, *smiles, takes off his glasses again, fiddles with them, smiles, puts them on, takes them off, puts them away. She tries to attract her husband's attention. But he hasn't noticed her, and is now joining in another round of the song.*)
Hey, you know, it's Friday! Jim, wait up, it's Friday; we've got customers! Hey!

---

* There are endless variations of this ridiculous but infectious professional ditty. They may be discovered not only among the Sappers but very widely in architectural, building and engineering circles.

TREDDLEHOYLE *turns round, fuddled, and seizes* RUTH *by
her two hands, spilling her drink.*

TREDDLEHOYLE (*with great emotion*). I'm going to have a new
shop! I'm going to have a right ritzy shop, and not a – not
a bleeding customer in the world!


*Treddlehoyle's fish shop: the wet-fish department.*
*The shop is still occupied by many customers with no one to serve
them. They are all listening in astonishment, as the singing in the
office continues.*
TREDDLEHOYLE *comes out to them, swaying slightly. He accosts
the* THIRD CUSTOMER.


TREDDLEHOYLE. Hurrah for the CRE . . . If I wor to tell
you we wor going to fix in here a glittering glass window and
a right bright glass door in the front of this shop, what'd
you reckon to that?

MISS HOOPER (*a sardonic old lady*). I'd reckon as price o' fish
wor going to go up.

*The song ends with a resounding chorus, and out they all troop
from the office.*
*They seem a little embarrassed by the stares of the shoppers.*

TREDDLEHOYLE. *I* warn't no sapper, you know, I wor the
Infantry of the Line, and if it warn't for the boys as built
the Bailey Bridges, we'd never have won the war!

GARNISH (*consolingly*). We wouldn't, Jim, we wouldn't. Well,
many thanks for your hospitality: and we'll see your job's
done as quickly as we can.

BARKER. Many thanks, Mr Treddlehoyle. Good morning.

TREDDLEHOYLE (*snatching the bottle from* DORIS). Hey, there's
still an inch left at the bottom . . .

PERKINS. No, thank you very much, sir: we've imposed on
you as it is. Very pleasant indeed. Good morning.

TREDDLEHOYLE (*pulling himself together*). Gentlemen, good morning. Good luck for the twenty-seventh.

*All the visitors leave.*

*The street outside Treddlehoyle's fish shop.*
*As they come out on to the pavement, the atmosphere of whisky and good fellowship evaporates in favour of one of brisk business.*
GARNISH *takes* BARKER *aside,* PERKINS *ditto with* RUTH.

GARNISH. Frank, just a minute . . .

PERKINS. If I come round on Monday, Miss Parsons, perhaps you and I could check through that specification again; there are one or two points about which I'm still not quite clear . . .

RUTH. Oh, yes, yes, I'll expect you – yes . . .

GARNISH. It's no use hoping for anything to open up over Prince Consort Street until the political side is properly squared. Right?

BARKER. Right.

GARNISH. So why don't you and your brother bring Alderman Butterthwaite to lunch at my club on Tuesday . . .

BARKER. Butterthwaite? You're flying a bit high there?

GARNISH. No, no, I know all about it. If we're to grip the Party, we have to grip it where it lives. So is it a date?

BARKER. I'll try, but I can't promise . . . It'd probably look better if *I* didn't come, though. Just you and Jerry and the Alderman. Bring me in later.

GARNISH. O.K. O.K. Then keep an hour clear. Other things being equal, you can join us over coffee.

BARKER. Right, I'll arrange it.

GARNISH. That's a good lad. And, er – do make sure *this* is a good job, won't you? He's a very old client, you see; he deserves the best.

BARKER. *And* he'll get it. Good-bye, Gilbert. Mr Perkins.

PERKINS. Be seeing you, Mr Barker. Mr Garnish, good morning.

GARNISH. Good morning.

(BARKER *and* PERKINS *disperse to their cars.*)

Right, Ruth. All well? We'll go back to the office. Quite a good morning's achievement, I think.

*Treddlehoyle's fish shop: the wet-fish department.*

FAT WOMAN (*to* DORIS). That wor a matey get-together, warn't it? I wish we could all do a day's work like that! Heh heh heh.

DORIS. It's all taken account of, love; it'll all be on the bill. (*She lowers her voice.*) But, you know, as far as my old man's back goes, I'd call it worth it. I wouldn't mind giving drinks to the whole of the Chamber of Commerce if it'd set him up straight again. Poor old devil: he's as stubborn as a goat!

*Garnish's drawing office.*
*All four at work.*

PERKINS *comes up to* RUTH'S *desk and deposits a brief-case on her drawing-board.*

PERKINS. I must confess to being a little worried about a point in your specification, Miss Parsons . . . er, here. (*He has taken the bound typescript from his brief-case and finds the place quickly.*)
Are you with me? The flooring to the W.C. Now, the drawing shows quite clearly a one-and-a-half-inch cement screed under the tiles. Is that really what you want?

RUTH. Oh yes, I think so. Isn't that right?

PERKINS. It's rather deep. We usually say three-quarter inch.

RUTH. Oh . . . I suppose it could be three-quarter inch. I can easily change it.

LESLIE *butts in without looking up from his work.*

LESLIE. Twice as thick means twice the price, dear.

PERKINS (*taking no notice*). If you use three-quarter inch, you'll find yourself with a three-quarter-inch step down into the toilet. Awkward dimension for a step that, too small to be noticed, but . . .

LESLIE (*as before*). Watch out, darling, you'll have old Treddle-hoyle falling base-over-apex into his own fitment. Heh!

RUTH *ignores him.* PERKINS *laughs primly.*

PERKINS. No step, then?

RUTH. No step.

PERKINS. In the specification, you never mentioned any screed at all.

RUTH. Oh.

PERKINS. We could insert it as an addendum.

RUTH. Yes, of course. Yes. We do have to have a screed, don't we?

PERKINS. It's usual . . . (*What he means is that it is not only usual, but imperative.*) And the other point I wanted to mention was, ah, yes: Page 33, *here*, you say 'In situ concrete window-cill, as per Detail Drawing No. 17'. We haven't had that drawing yet, have we?

RUTH. Yes, I – er – I'll be working on it this afternoon.

PERKINS. Good. Thank you very much, Miss Parsons. Better not to have any ambiguities. Particularly as our friend Mr Barker, perhaps . . . I'll be on my way. Good morning.

(PERKINS *goes out.* PETER *gets up from his work and comes over to* RUTH.)

PETER. You want to get your Spess and your drawings dead accurate, you know: all tied up. No loopholes. Barker's a shark.

RUTH. I thought he seemed rather pleasant. (APPLEYARD *returns to his desk.*) He was watching Mrs Treddlehoyle. A melancholy seducer. He took off his spectacles when he thought she was looking at him.

KRANK *quietly takes off his.*

LESLIE. The raging passions in the breasts of the moneyed men of this city are nobody's business. I could tell you some tales. Look at this heart-breaking piece of Amalgamated Corn I've been destroying my integrity with for the last six months!
(*He gestures angrily at his perspective of the Quicksnack office, a print of which has been pinned up on the wall above his drawing-board.*)
The Quicksnack Super Breakfast. And you know what cooked it up, don't you? A quite unofficial but delicious bit of snackery between greedy Gibby Garnish and Harry Sweetman's madam in the back of his Bentley!

RUTH (*properly sceptical*). I don't believe a word of it.

LESLIE. Come on, Mr Appleyard, I'm off for my lunch.

PETER. It's not time.

LESLIE. It is.

PETER (*looking at his watch*). It isn't . . . Hallo, you're not wrong, you're right though: it's just on. Bide a moment . . .
(*He puts the finishing touches to the line he is drawing.*)
*There* . . . Right, we're away.

LESLIE *and* PETER *take their coats and leave the office rapidly.*

KRANK. You go for lunch, Ruth?

RUTH. Sandwiches.

*She takes out of her string bag a packet of salami sandwiches and some lettuce and a raw carrot.*

KRANK. Ah. Very sensible. I, too. Polish salami.
(*He takes his sandwiches out of his holdall, and brings them over beside her.*)

We are a passionate nation, you know, but *cold* and passionate, that's no good.

RUTH (*seriously*). I'm half-Russian, you know.

KRANK. No? What part of Russia?

RUTH. What part? Oh . . . I'm not really sure, you see. My grandmother used to tell me that . . .

KRANK. Maternal grandmother?

RUTH. Yes.

KRANK. Good! Very good! Always through the line of the female comes the true heart of the spirit. Tell me, why did you think you ought to be an architect?

RUTH. What? I don't know, really.

KRANK. You don't know?

RUTH. Well, it seemed interesting, when I was at school. I thought that I . . .

KRANK. You thought that you would be responsible for creating beautiful and fabulous structures to delight the heart of man? Today, I call myself a Practical Man. Me and Peter Appleyard: twin brothers in Practicality. I said to myself: Architecture is building. Building is a Quintessential of Life (philosophical term) and for Quintessentials men will pay. Now then, your fish shop: how old is the building?

RUTH. It was a Victorian house originally.

KRANK. Aha, very good. Adaptability and Practicality. The genius for English Compromise. This is the first important contract you have yourself handled, is it not? Now, when Mr Garnish goes to Paris, you may feel you are in difficulties with it a little: you ask me: I will help you out.

RUTH (*in alarm*). Paris? Who says he's going to Paris?

KRANK. Next week: oh yes, he's going. There are possibilities, I believe, of an English factory for a big French industrial group – Anyway, he hopes for the job. If he gets it, he will be most preoccupied back and forward to the airport every week of the month. So you will be on your own! Peter Appleyard: don't ask *him*. He is too reliable. What you will need is the power of imagination. This fish shop is to be *our* fish shop, alone. A little jewel, you see, among the tenements of the Intake Road. Don't let Peter spoil it.

RUTH. Oh dear . . . I hope it's going to be all right.

KRANK. I tell you: it will be beautiful. You will, for the first time, create.

(*They are now getting warm.* KRANK *is close beside her. One arm comes round her, and with the other he removes his glasses, which he had put on again to look at her drawing.*)

Ah, you are such a bud of a flower, Ruth: I should like to see you open . . .

(*The telephone rings.*)

I think it is for me.

*But* RUTH *has got to it first – he being preoccupied with his glasses.*

RUTH (*on the telephone*). Yes . . . yes, he's here . . .

*She turns to* KRANK, *round-eyed.*

It's a woman.

KRANK. A woman? Aha . . . (*He takes the receiver.*) Hallo-allo . . . Speaking . . . No, that is most unwise, Teresa. I do not recommend it . . .

(*He glances covertly at* RUTH *as he talks, to watch her reaction.*)

Teresa, I said No. If the police are asking questions, you must answer them properly and behave like a responsible citizen. To run away to Doncaster would be to bring about the most serious trouble and I do not permit it . . . No no, no no no, do as I tell you and do not ring me here again! Good-bye.

(*He rings off crossly, and meditates for a moment: then comes over to* RUTH, *very seriously.*)

Ah, Ruth, you must be very careful. I am not a man to do you any good. I am too involved with too many difficult businesses. I do not *want* to be involved. And above all, not my friends. No no. *You* are my friend. Do not be led into temptation.

RUTH (*tremendously excited by all this performance*). The police! What do they want? You don't mean you're – mixed up in . . . perhaps you're in a gang?

KRANK (*with sudden real sincerity*). Certainly not! I do not approve of any form of violence. I am going out now for some milk from the slot-machine. Can I get you some?

RUTH. I'll come down with you.

KRANK. No no. If you please. In the street it is better if I am – inconspicuous? . . . Remember, you must not be – involved.

*He has put on his hat and coat all in one movement, and taking up his holdall, slides out of the room.*
*She looks after him, very impressed.*

*Treddlehoyle's fish shop: the wet-fish department.*
*A good deal of confusion.*
WORKMEN *are bringing in enormous quantities of their apparatus and materials for the building, passing and repassing between the shop and the street. Two of them, singing 'When Father Papered the Parlour', come through with a number of long planks carried between them. They barge through the wet-fish area and dump their load down across the door leading to the frying department.*
DORIS, *dodging about the place, trying to keep an eye on things, endeavours to intercept them.*

DORIS. Hey, steady on, don't put it there! Jim!

TREDDLEHOYLE *comes out of the office with a bundle of invoices and a bad temper.*

TREDDLEHOYLE. What's the matter?

DORIS. Tell 'em they can't put it here. They're blocking the door up.

TREDDLEHOYLE *speaks to a passing* WORKMAN, *in vain.*

TREDDLEHOYLE. Hey, wait up, wait up a second; don't put this lot here – you're blocking the door up – I can't get at me fish fryer . . .

FIRST WORKMAN. Better ask the foreman, lad. *I* don't know nowt about it.

TREDDLEHOYLE. Foreman?

SECOND WORKMAN. He said, chuck it down here, he said. You'd better ask him.

TREDDLEHOYLE. Where is he?

THIRD WORKMAN. What?

TREDDLEHOYLE. Where's the foreman?

THIRD WORKMAN. Which one?

TREDDLEHOYLE. How many are there?

FIRST WORKMAN. Foreman joiner's not on the job yet.

TREDDLEHOYLE. Well, who *is* on the job?

SECOND WORKMAN. What?

TREDDLEHOYLE. Who told you to put this lot here?

SECOND WORKMAN. Bob Ackroyd.

TREDDLEHOYLE. Who's he?

SECOND WORKMAN. General foreman. You want to ask him.


*The street outside Treddlehoyle's fish shop.*
*The* FOREMAN, *a sombre, slow-spoken, deep-eyed pessimist, is checking his list of stores as they are unloaded – if possible, we should see the tail of the lorry and stuff being lifted off it.*
*The* FIRST WORKMAN *comes up for instructions.*


FOREMAN. That's about the lot, then. What's happened to that Flannigan or whatever his name is?

FIRST WORKMAN. Flannigan?

FOREMAN. Well, Flannigan, Bannigan, Monahan . . .

FIRST WORKMAN. Oh, you mean the Irisher. He's stopped off a minute.

FOREMAN. Then he'd better stop on again or I'll have him off it for good. Send him in to me as soon as he comes.

(TREDDLEHOYLE *has come out and is standing at the* FOREMAN'S *elbow, trying to get a word in.*

*The* FOREMAN *becomes aware of him.*)

Hello, who are you?

TREDDLEHOYLE. My name's Treddlehoyle . . .

FOREMAN (*preoccupied with his schedules*). Aye, and you look like it and all. Are you on this job?

TREDDLEHOYLE. On it! I'm *paying* for it!

FOREMAN (*only very slightly disconcerted*). Eh? . . . Oh . . . Good afternoon.

(*He continues talking to the* FIRST WORKMAN.)

And what about them four-by-two's? I told you to see they wor here. And they're not. Where are they?

FIRST WORKMAN. Mr Harrison said tomorrow . . .

FOREMAN. Then Mr Harrison can damn well go and – all right . . . I'll sort it.

TREDDLEHOYLE. You're blocking up my door.

FOREMAN. What?

TREDDLEHOYLE. I can't get into the frying department.

FOREMAN. Frying. I want to have a look at that. This the way?

*He goes into the shop without a backward glance, via the separate door into the frying department.*

*Treddlehoyle's shop: the frying department.*
*The* FOREMAN *comes in from the street as* DORIS *clambers over the planks from the wet-fish department.*
*She is carrying a tray of cod, to prepare for frying.*

FOREMAN (*briefly*). Afternoon.

DORIS (*even more briefly*). I know it's afternoon. We expected you this morning.

*She puts the cod on the counter and starts to work with the knife.*

FOREMAN (*with prophetic relish*). I dare say you did, missus. Continued disappointment is the lot of the human race. Is this the fish fryer?

TREDDLEHOYLE (*who has followed him in*). That's right.

*The* FOREMAN *looking at his schedule and the plan he has.*

FOREMAN. Wait a minute: let's check . . . Right! That's the fish-fryer. Here's where we start. Taylor, Jorkins: get this shifted!
(*The* FIRST *and* SECOND WORKMEN *come in from the wet-fish department, and immediately start to work, unplugging electric leads, etc.*)
Where's that Brannigan!

*A* FOURTH WORKMAN, *a young Irishman, carrying a pick, comes in from the wet-fish department.*

FOURTH WORKMAN. Here I am, sir. I'm sorry for the delay now, but . . .

FOREMAN. Have you got your pick?

FOURTH WORKMAN. I have.

FOREMAN. Then get moving on these floortiles. I want 'em all up by tea-time.

FOURTH WORKMAN. Right you are, sir. All o' them up.

*He starts picking vigorously at the floortiles.*

TREDDLEHOYLE (*knuckling under with what philosophy he can command*). Well, I'm the paymaster. I suppose I've to put up with it . . . Doris, where's the blackboard? Seems to me there's going to be more of a muck-up than I'd took account of. He's cracking up the floor and all?

FOREMAN. Got to be done.

TREDDLEHOYLE. Eh dear . . .

DORIS *piles up her cod again to take them out.*
*The* FOURTH WORKMAN *recommences his labour.*
TREDDLEHOYLE *takes the blackboard, on which is chalked
'Frying tonight at six', rubs out the last two words and writes
'No' at the top, then puts it in the window.*


*Barker's office.*
BARKER *is on the telephone.*

BARKER. Hello, can I speak to Mr Garnish, please ? Barker of
Durable here . . . Hello, sir, is that you ? . . . Excuse the
melodrama, but is there anybody with you ? . . . Right,
we can talk. That little lunch-party of yours, y'know: I
think you've pulled it off! The – er – as we might term it,
the grapevine from City Hall dropped a bunch of very ripe
fruit on my desk this morning. Butterthwaite is switching the
party line! . . . He *is*! He *is*! Of course, it'll take him a
week or two – he's got to be dead careful he don't make it
look like collusion with the Conservatives: but . . . when
are you back from Paris ? . . . Fine. Now, if you can get
your lads right away on revising the old drawings, we can
bang 'em straight in to City Hall in time for the next Planning Committee on the fifteenth prox . . . and Prince Consort Street is *ours*! . . . It's very kind of you to say so, Mr
Garnish. Thank you. By the way, about Mr Treddlehoyle's
fish shop, there *was* one small point . . .


*Garnish's drawing-office.*
KRANK *is absent.*
*The other three are standing around drinking tea.*
GARNISH *bursts in.*

GARNISH. Morning all. There's a big flap on. Now, what's
everybody doing ? Don't tell me: I can see. Just break up the

tea-party for two minutes and let's have your attention, please. Peter, can that bus station take care of itself for a fortnight?

PETER. I think so, Mr Garnish.

GARNISH. Right. Now I want you to go down to the basement and look out the old drawings for the redevelopment of Prince Consort Street, the job that never came off. Remember?

PETER. Yes, sir. 1953. Durable were planning it as a speculation?

GARNISH. That's right. Well: it's *coming* off, now. When you've found them, bring 'em in to my office. Leslie, I want you on this as well. You can leave that snap-crackle-pop to its digestion and get on with something dynamic. We'd better have Krank on it, too . . . where *is* he?

PETER. Gone on a site-visit, I believe. City Hall Canteen.

GARNISH (*grunts*). He would have. Well, hurry it up, boys; I've got a plane to catch this afternoon. Ruth, Mr Barker wants a word with you about some snag that's cropped up at the Intake Road. When you've had your lunch, you can take the bus there: meet him on the site at half past two. Will you do that?

RUTH. Yes, Mr Garnish.

GARNISH. Good . . . all right, all right, hurry it up, then.

*He dashes out, slamming the door behind him.*

*Treddlehoyle's fish shop: the frying department.*
*This has been completely gutted, the equipment moved, the floor up. The appalling litter of the contractor is piled about in the corners.*
*The* FOURTH WORKMAN, *whistling 'When Father Papered the Parlour', is chopping experimentally at the wall dividing this half of the shop from the wet-fish department.*

*He chops a little carelessly and three or four bricks suddenly fall
out of the wall at a height of about five feet.*
*In the hole thus created, the gloomy face of* TREDDLEHOYLE
*is seen framed.*

TREDDLEHOYLE. Nay, if I couldn't do better nor that, I'd
   give over . . .
   (*The* FOURTH WORKMAN *smiles and gives him a pleasant
   salute.*)
   Look, I'm *trying* to serve my customers.

TREDDLEHOYLE *turns away in annoyance.*


*Treddlehoyle's fish shop: the wet-fish department.*
*We see that* TREDDLEHOYLE *is serving fish from a makeshift
counter along one side of a narrow passage framed with softboard,
which is all that the builders have left him.*
*His back is to the wall in which the* WORKMAN *has knocked the
hole.*
*There is a queue of jostling women.*
TREDDLEHOYLE *turns round from the hole and remonstrates
with his customers.*

TREDDLEHOYLE. All right, ladies, now take it easy, please.
   One at a time, please, one at a time!
   (*He speaks more confidentially to the woman at the front, as
   he wraps and weighs her fish.*)
   It wor supposed to *cure* my rheumatism, this lot! That do
   you? Two and three . . . next lady, if you please.
   (*The* SECOND WORKMAN *comes out of the innards of the shop,
   pushing a wheelbarrow full of rubble.*)
SECOND WORKMAN. Mind your backs, please!

*He forces his way past the customers towards the opening to the
street, where he meets* RUTH.

*She tries to avoid him, but he, trying to avoid her, only obstructs
her again.*
*There is an awkward moment of mutual dodging.*

RUTH. Sorry, I – er – is Mr Barker on the site yet?
SECOND WORKMAN. Who?

BARKER *appears at the far end of the shop, signalling to* RUTH
*over the heads of the customers.*

BARKER. Hello! Here! Miss – er . . .
RUTH (*waving back*). Oh, hello . . . I – er . . . coming . . .
(*She forces her way into the building. As she passes* TREDDLE-
HOYLE.)
Good afternoon, Mr Treddlehoyle.
TREDDLEHOYLE (*wanting to speak to her*). Good afternoon
. . . Hey, miss . . .

*But she has gone past him, flustered: and he mutters crossly as
he returns to his work.*


*Treddlehoyle's fish shop: the frying department.*
RUTH *and* BARKER *come in from the back of the wet-fish over a
heap of rubble and shovels.*
*The* FOREMAN *also appears from the recesses and joins them.*
*The* FOURTH WORKMAN *is still picking at the wall.*

BARKER. Sorry to bring you up from the office so soon after
lunch, Miss – er . . .
RUTH. Parsons.
BARKER (*taking off his glasses and putting them on again*).
Parsons, of course . . . I was on the blower to Mr Garnish,
you see – he's off to France tomorrow, isn't he?
RUTH. This afternoon.
BARKER. Ey-ey, stopping overnight in Paris? Wish I could

pick up some o' *my* business in that part of the world, eh? Ha-ha . . .

(*He takes off his glasses again in rapid embarrassment.*)

Right, well, the point I had at issue was this . . . we've been excavating across the whole front of the shop to set in the drain for these floor-gullies of yours. Have you got the drawing, Bob?

*The* FOREMAN *hands him a dog-eared drawing.*

FOREMAN. Here.

BARKER. So you see what we've come up against.

(*The* FOREMAN *has crooked his finger to the* FOURTH WORKMAN, *who helps him lift away a plank on the ground at the front of the shop, revealing a trench.*

RUTH *looks into it with an attempt at wisdom.*)

Well, where would you like us to lay the drain, Miss Parsons?

RUTH. The drain . . .

BARKER (*replacing his glasses*). Can I make a suggestion?

RUTH. Oh yes, yes, do, please.

BARKER. There's a ten-inch discrepancy to start with, then another eleven and a half for the pier, that makes one foot nine and a half – *that's* all right, we can turn it round at the end with an eighth-circle bend-section and run it into your trapped-gully as afore said; *but* the level's affected, isn't it? Has to be. What about your minimum slab?

RUTH. Could we raise the floor? I mean, a couple of inches.

BARKER. Bob?

FOREMAN. No problem there. We'd just augment the hardcore. It means the step up to your front door's increased, when you come in.

RUTH. Yes. I don't suppose that matters.

FOREMAN. Whatever you say, miss. What about the W.C.?

RUTH. The W.C.!

FOREMAN. We've laid the slab already. It'll mean a two-inch step down.

BARKER (*takes off his glasses*). We could increase the screed.

RUTH. Yes . . . Do you think that would be all right?

BARKER. Bob?

FOREMAN. No, no, you've to tell *us*, miss. You're the architect.

RUTH. Yes . . . Yes, well, I think we will do that.

FOREMAN. Increase the screed.

RUTH. That's right.

FOREMAN. Have to have that in writing.

BARKER (*fiddling with his glasses*). I suppose it's too late for Mr Garnish to get us out a letter tonight with a proper Variation Order?

RUTH. I think he'll have left for the airport by now. But I can send you the letter myself.

BARKER (*putting on his glasses*). Splendid. Can you start that right away, Bob?

FOREMAN. Right.

BARKER. Good afternoon, then. So long, Bob.

BARKER *goes out, straight into the street, by pushing aside the temporary canvas that has replaced the front window of the frying department.*

RUTH *looks round, a little nervously. Her eye falls on a three-quarters completed brick column that is to support the ceiling.*

RUTH. How's the bricklaying going, Mr Ackroyd?

FOREMAN. All right, miss. We've set it up as far as we can go for the time.

RUTH. I see. How much more do you have to do?

FOREMAN. Set in your formwork, lay on your RSJ, cast in the casing, *then* we can set about doing the rest of your bricks. No point going through Liverpool if you want to get to Sheffield – is there?

(*The* FOREMAN *suddenly becomes very confidential, looks round to see that the four workmen are not listening, takes* RUTH *aside.*)

Excuse me asking you this, won't you? But I take it your

firm are the ones what our people are connected with in regard to the Prince Consort Street site?

RUTH. I think so.

FOREMAN. Aye. It'll be a big contract.

RUTH. I should think so, yes –

FOREMAN. Has anything been said yet about appointing a General Foreman?

RUTH (*blankly astonished*). Why, I haven't the faintest idea!

FOREMAN (*erupting with unexpected bitterness*). You haven't? I thought you architects knew the lot, with your college educations. I'm about sick of these meddling little jobs! But does Sharkey Barker give a pig's rivet for what *I* think? Look who he's put in charge of that damn great bus terminal contract!

RUTH. Who?

FOREMAN. Jack Hickleton, that's who! I knew him when he wor a snot-nosed nipper chucking fireworks into my back-garden . . . Oooh, it fair curdles you up, dunnit? . . . But I don't suppose there's nowt *you* can do about it. Excuse my verbosity . . . Hey, Donovan, if you lean on that pick any longer, it'll sink into the ground and you'll be charged for it's replacement!

*He moves savagely back into the back of the building.*
*The* FOURTH WORKMAN *grins at* RUTH.
TREDDLEHOYLE'S *face is once more framed in the aperture.*

TREDDLEHOYLE. Excuse me, Miss Parsons. Can I have a word. Here –
(*He beckons* RUTH *over to the hole and talks earnestly to her.*)
It's not right, you know, it's not right at all. Mr Garnish gave me his affydavy as the work would be planned to cause the minimum inconvenience. They wor his own straight words, Miss Parsons: and now look at it! I want to know who's responsible. You tell Mr Garnish I want him to

telephone me personal this afternoon and I want satisfaction.

RUTH. I'm afraid he's gone to Paris.

TREDDLEHOYLE. Paris!

*DORIS has come in to the frying department from behind*
*RUTH.*

DORIS. You don't want to take no notice, love. He's been kicking against this job ever since it began. It *is* going all right, isn't it?

RUTH. Oh yes, Mrs Treddlehoyle, really it is . . .

DORIS. That's right, then. You don't need to bother Mr Garnish. *I'll* sort it out.


*Garnish's private office.*

GARNISH *enters in his outdoor clothes, slams a thick brief-case on his desk, throws off his Anthony Eden hat, sits down at the desk, groans, looks at a pile of letters waiting for him, holds his head in his hands, sits up, buzzes on his intercom.*

GARNISH (*into intercom*). Miss Waters! . . . Miss Waters!
. . . oh.
(*There being no answer, he turns to the letters and starts leafing through them with distaste. There is a knock at the door.*)
Come!
(*The* TEA-MAN *enters with a cup of tea.*)
Hello. What can I do for you, Herbert?

TEA-MAN. I took it you was back from Paris, sir. I just saw you come in.

GARNISH. Did you? Nobody else did. What's happened to Miss Waters?

TEA-MAN. They say she wor poorly.

GARNISH. What, again?
*He is looking incredulously at a hand-written letter on a heavily printed tradesman's notepaper.*

TEA-MAN. Ah, she's getting to the age. It struck me *you* wor looking a bit rough and all. I thought you'd want a break with your rule for once and have a cup o' tea. I brought it.

GARNISH. What, tea? You know I never have . . . oh, my God, I *will* have it! And I'll have these as well!

*He swallows a couple of pills and takes a gulp of tea.*

TEA-MAN. You see, I thought you looked a bit rough. I thought . . . the Paris plane, it must have been bumpy. Was I right?

GARNISH. You were . . . you know, you're very solicitous all of a sudden. What's your motives?

TEA-MAN. Motives? I've got no motives.

GARNISH *buzzes again. This time there is an answer.*

GARNISH. Hello, who's there? Why is there nobody there? Doreen! Is that you? . . . Look, if Miss Waters is ill, who's going to do my letters? You? . . . Right. You can start off by sending me in – oh whatshername, with the untidy hair – little Miss Parsons. I want a word with her.

GARNISH *finishes his conversation on the intercom, to find the* TEA-MAN *waiting about.*

Well?

TEA-MAN. It's a matter, you see, about these tea-trays for the top-floor offices. What about my disability? I can't undertake to carry them up more nor the basement flight.

GARNISH. You've carried them up every day for three years without collapsing.

TEA-MAN. I'm on the Schedule of Disabled Persons, Mr Garnish, look it's wrote in my card . . .

GARNISH. I know, I know: all right, all right, you can leave your trays in future at the corner of the passage and you can tell the assistants if they want any tea they can carry it up themselves. Satisfied?

TEA-MAN. Mr Garnish, I'm very much obliged . . .

GARNISH (*irritated almost beyond bearing*). Don't say it . . .

TEA-MAN. No, sir, I will say it: and all of us old Sappers what served in Works Services Madagascar could never use another word. Colonel Garnish, we used to say, is a *gentleman*: and your command, sir, was a demi-paradise!

GARNISH. That just about describes it . . . Take this out with you.

*Thrusts the empty cup at the* TEA-MAN, *who backs to the door as* RUTH *enters.*

TEA-MAN. Thank *you*, Mr Garnish. The compliment still holds, sir.

*He leaves and* RUTH *stands waiting, while* GARNISH *looks at some letters. He suddenly glares up at her.*

GARNISH. I am back from Paris. Good morning. Prince Consort Street, now: is it all done?

RUTH. I don't really know. Peter seems to be getting on quite fast with it, but . . .

GARNISH. What about you?

RUTH. *I'm* not on Prince Consort Street.

GARNISH. I *know* you're not on Consort Street. I said Intake Road . . .

(*He flourishes the letter.*)

What the devil's this? I can't read a word this morning . . . round and round and round. You read it to me.

RUTH (*looking at the letter*). It's from Mr Treddlehoyle.

GARNISH. It's from Mr Treddlehoyle.

RUTH (*reading it*). He says: 'Dear Mr Garnish, I write as per your young lady's recent visit to this address. I am indeed sorry to have forgotten myself and made use of an abusive criticism. I now realize all is according to plan except where unavoidable, and so I am truly sorry for any offence taken. I put my fullest trust in you, Mr Garnish, as ever, and hope that there are no hard feelings. Yours truly, J. K. Treddle-hoyle. PS. Will you ask Miss Parsons to let me know what is to be done about unfinished brickwork. They seem to be leaving it just as it stands and I am very concerned.'

GARNISH. All right. I don't know whose fault all this was: but for God's sake watch yourself when you're dealing with Jim Treddlehoyle. Put it quite bluntly; he's an ignorant old man, and he has to be nursed. Here he is, look, with his roof in, his floor up, and he doesn't know what's hit him. So be gentle – Sweet, soothing, sympathetic . . . Oh yes, Variation Orders.

(*He ruffles through a pile of letters in his tray.*)

You seem to have been dishing 'em out this week like a regular paper chase. I'm trusting you to know enough about it to be sure that all of them were needed . . . but on a good job there's none needed. Right? All right. Oh my head goes round and round . . .

*Garnish's drawing-office.*
*Lunch-time.* KRANK *is alone in the room, talking on the telephone.*

KRANK. All right, very good, I am satisfied, yes . . . Now listen to me, Teresa, the most important thing is you must change your accommodation. Once a house becomes known to the police it is no good at all continuing the game there. I have acquired a very attractive and convenient premises at the top of the Intake Road, and Gromek is coming round with the van this afternoon to convey your possessions . . . Don't argue, my sweetheart, I am the landlord: I say you will move . . . O.K. Be contented. (*Kisses.*) You are the most beautiful of them all. Good-bye.

KRANK *rings off and takes a drink from a carton of milk.*
PETER *comes in, rubbing his hands happily, followed by* LESLIE, *who looks unhappy and sits sulkily at his desk.*

PETER. Hello, where's Ruth gone?

KRANK. She had to go to a site-visit, I believe. There is a great
deal of trouble up the Intake Road. The Local Authority
Building Inspector, he arrived unexpectedly, and – oh, my
goodness, the bureaucracy! Left hand, right hand, tear it
down, pull it out, condemn it! You have had a good lunch
at the self-service cafeteria?

PETER. Not bad. They do a very nice steak pie. But they've
no idea at all how to make a cup of tea. Not fit for nowt but
washing out the drain.

KRANK. Ah, you should drink your tea with lemon. In a glass.
Beautiful.

PETER. Ugh . . . Well, it looks like Prince Consort Street is
clear.

KRANK. Clear?

PETER (*with enthusiasm*). That's right. They've given us the
go-ahead. Barker's gang of layabouts are starting in tomorrow. Lovely grub. Demolition of thirteen shops, two blocks
of offices, one detached house, and a Methody Chapel.
Clear, sheer, and away: for Appleyard's grand project!

LESLIE (*sourly*). Appleyard for king!

PETER. Well, I don't see why not – at the rate the stocks and
shares are going to go up for Durable out o' this, and the
turnover of the floor rentals rolling in, and all . . .

KRANK. You should ask Mr Garnish to increase your salary.

PETER. Well, y'know, by rights – I've a jolly good mind.

LESLIE. You must be off your nut.

KRANK. I must go to the City Hall to have a look at my canteen. The ventilation ducting is not yet quite decided.
Good-bye.

*He goes out.*

*Treddlehoyle's fish shop: frying department.*

*In much the same state as the last scene here, but more so.*
RUTH *and the* FOREMAN *are in earnest consultation.*

RUTH. But he can't make us pull down the whole roof!
FOREMAN. He can.
RUTH. Why, it'll cost thousands!
FOREMAN. Such are the risks taken, Miss Parsons, with indiscriminate mucking-about on an old structure. That roof wor never touched at the first alterations, wor it?
RUTH. I don't suppose it was.
FOREMAN. There you are then – storage up of trouble for future posterity. He rebuilds the shop without attention to the rafters. Twenty years after, your Building Inspector discovers the dry-rot and condemns the whole roof. All quite predictable: but where wor the voice of warning in 1938?

*He leads the way to the back of the shop, where the door through to the wet-fish and the stairs has been removed and replaced by some soft boarding and a canvas flap.*
*The* FOREMAN *goes through the flap and up the stairs.*
*As* RUTH *is about to follow him* DORIS *appears round the temporary partitioning from the wet-fish counter.*

DORIS. What's the matter?
RUTH. The matter?
DORIS. There's summat up, ent there? I saw that little fox-terrier from City Hall prowling around this morning with his brief-case and black bowler. Jim's away today – what have I got to tell him when he comes home to his tea?
RUTH. I haven't really looked at it yet, Mrs Treddlehoyle – I don't think it can be anything very serious – technical reasons, you know, up in the roof.
DORIS. Like, the water-pipes, and that?

*A cry off:* 'Shop!'

RUTH. I'll tell you more about it when I've been and had a look – Mr Ackroyd's gone up – I'm coming, Mr Ackroyd!

*She escapes up the stairs. Cry again:* 'Shop!'

DORIS. All right, I can hear you. We're not made of wood.


*Treddlehoyle's fish shop: under the roof.*
*A cramped little loft between the first-floor ceiling and the rafters, occupied chiefly by the water-tank.*
*A small dirty skylight in the slope of the roof.*
*A hatch in the floor, through which the* FOREMAN *climbs, followed by* RUTH. *As he comes up, he gives her one hand to help her, and smacks at the rafters with the other.*

FOREMAN. You see, all o' this wood's got the rot creeping through it. Look at this here . . . you might be ripping up asbestos. There's worm in the purlins, and all. What I might term an unavoidable misfortune. Well, I dare say you'll want to take a survey of the existing condition, so I'll leave you to it. I was on one o' these conversion jobs once; they took out one brick, the whole back wall came down on top of the foreman carpenter and had him into hospital for the best of eight month. Heh, we ought to call ourselves lucky, we ought . . .

*He descends through the hatch.*
RUTH *sits for a moment, gloomily humming 'When Father Papered the Parlour', singing the words at the lines:*
RUTH (*singing*). 'You never saw such a stuck-up family so stuck up before.'

*Then she pulls herself together, takes out her equipment and starts to work. She moves about in the loft, examining the timbers, humming the tune, and clearly not knowing where to begin. At intervals she taps the woodwork as if by so doing she*

*could know whether it is sound or not. She obviously does not
know. Suddenly she hears an answering tap. She taps again.
There is another answer.*

*She hums again, and she hears the tune taken up by another
voice.*

*She taps rapidly to find out where this is coming from, and is
answered rapidly by taps which she traces to the triangular
wall of the loft, where it obviously abuts on the next house.*

*A hitherto unnoticed trap-door in this wall opens, and* KRANK'S
*head emerges.*

KRANK. Hello! How are you? Here am I.

(*He clambers through.*)

Extraordinary coincidence. Aha, but not without a rational
explanation. It is no accident that I am here . . . So they
have condemned your roof, have they? Has it occurred to
you, my dear, that if these timbers are rotten the ones of the
coeval and adjacent buildings are likely to be likewise?

RUTH. I just do *not* know what you think you're up to!

KRANK. We will come to that later. The immediate issue is as
follows: this roof and the contiguous roofs are basically the
one structure. If there is to be reconstruction, it will clearly
be more economical to do both together as an integral project. No?

RUTH. It might be . . . it would depend upon the owner of
the property . . . Who *is* the owner of the property?

KRANK. Next door? Me. Next door *that* way? Me, too. All
within the last week, very fast worker.

RUTH. I should just think you are . . .

KRANK. Aha, my little flower, it is all for the fun of the game,
is it not? What game? Oh, Ruth, sometimes even *I* cannot
tell you *that* answer.

KRANK *sits down and starts to sing, quietly and personally, as
if he is telling her a secret.*

*The tune is 'When Father Papered the Parlour'.*

*(Singing).*

    'A house is built of timber
    And bricks and bits of iron.
    You build up a house,
    You build up another,
    Hundreds of houses all together.
    Two hundred make you a street, dear,
    Ten thousand make you a town,
    And all the breath of the land of England,
    Is smothering under the ground.'

Of course, you and I are not entirely under the ground, *we* are in an attic, with one little skylight, from which if it pleased us and if it were cleaned, we could take a view out over the whole of this city, but it does not at the moment please me, so let it remain obscured. They believe I am visiting the City Hall, so I do not have to be back at the office for another fifty minutes. And you have your measurements to take, have you not? If it pleases you, Ruth, and you are in any way pressed for time, I will be so happy to help you to take them . . .

*He strokes her face softly.*
*He takes off her spectacles: and she, his.*

*Treddlehoyle's fish shop: the wet-fish department.*
*The cramped-in space we have already seen.*
DORIS *is at the counter, serving a customer* (MRS HIGSON).
TREDDLEHOYLE *enters from the street, boisterously.*

TREDDLEHOYLE. Hello, hello, there! Shop! How are you Mrs Higson? Now don't you tell me you're poorly, not today, no, you're not! You don't look it, I won't believe it, I won't hear of it, you're as ruddy as a rosebud.
MRS HIGSON. I'm glad there's somebody as thinks so.

*She goes out with her fish.*

DORIS. What makes you so brisk and sparky?

TREDDLEHOYLE. I've gone daft, I'm clear barmy, I've blown five hundred pounds!

DORIS. What on?

TREDDLEHOYLE. New fish fryer, chip compartment, hotplate, double aluminium sink, waste disposal and service bar, all in the one unit. I've just been down to the electricity showrooms . . and they've caught me, you know, they've made a right muggins out o' me. It's fair lovely, it is. Gilbert Garnish has been after me for months to buy it, but I couldn't like come round to it at first. It seemed such a lot . . . Well, I've changed me mind! And here's a little summat, like, to be going on with. I got this one for *you*.

*He takes out from behind his back, where he has been hiding it coyly, a bright new omelette pan made of copper.*

DORIS. Oh, Jim, I'm that glad! I'm that relieved! You don't know how much I've been wanting you to go for that fish fryer.

TREDDLEHOYLE. Here, let's have a smacker on the gobber . . .

*He takes her to give her a large kiss.*
*We see that in the shadows at the back of the shop the* FORE-MAN *is sitting on an upturned bucket, drinking a cup of tea.*
KRANK *comes down the stairs and passes through the shop and out into the street.*

KRANK (*en passant*). Excuse me, thank you, I am just passing through. Good afternoon.

RUTH *comes down the stairs after him.*

RUTH (*very flustered*). Oh it's all right, he's from the office with me. I'd better send you a letter from the office when we've worked it all out. We're not quite clear just yet of the exact implications . . . Good-bye.

*She hurries out into the street.*

TREDDLEHOYLE. Well.

> *The* FOREMAN *clears his throat, wipes his mouth and comes forward.*

*A bus shelter.*
*This is a long seat with a back to it and a roof over. Bus time-tables posted up inside.*
MRS HIGSON *is sitting at one end of the seat.* KRANK *and* RUTH *arrive in a hurry.*

RUTH. I think we've missed it.
KRANK. There should be another one. Excuse me, dear lady, is there please a bus for the city centre?
MRS HIGSON. You want a number ten.
KRANK. Yes.

> MRS HIGSON *suddenly realizes she is talking to a foreigner, becomes painfully explicit.*

MRS HIGSON. What you want is a number *ten*. Every *five* minutes. You do understand, don't you? You can see it, *number ten*: up on the *front*.
KRANK. Yes, yes: I thank you.

> *He sits down with* RUTH *at the far end of the seat from* MRS HIGSON.
> RUTH *puts her head on his shoulder.*

RUTH. Poor Mr Treddlehoyle.
KRANK. It can scarcely be avoided, I am afraid . . . Old houses will fall down . . . You understand me, Ruth, this is not to be remembered, what took place this afternoon. It is not to be cried for.
RUTH. I am not crying.

KRANK. Oh, but I think you are. What is this?

*He picks off a tear from her cheek with his finger, gently.*

RUTH (*half laughing*). I am allowed to be romantic. I'm supposed to be an artist.

KRANK. Ah yes, that is true. But always let your intelligence
control it, you see. Regard me as I am: a man with neither
brick nor timber that I myself have put together. (*He begins
to sing again, very softly.*)

> 'Before I came from Poland
> I filled a sack with earth:
> I wanted it shown,
> I needed it known,
> Wherever I went I'd still be at home.
> But they covered the road with barbed wire:
> It was all I could do to get through.
> My earth was scattered across the wind
> And my sack was torn in two.'

So now, you see, all that I can do is to accommodate myself
to the disciplines, the religions, the prejudicial customs of
whatever people I might chance to fall in with. Thus, I can
live. Otherwise . . .
(KRANK *shrugs. Suddenly he whips off his hat and hides his
face behind it.*) Psst! Pretend I'm not here. (*A shadow passes
across them as someone moves slowly in front of the shelter.*
KRANK *sits up again, puts back his hat on his head, and breathes
a sigh of relief.*)
A policeman. I knew his face. Just a possibility he might
have known mine.

RUTH. Here comes a bus. It looks like . . .

KRANK. Yes, I think it is.

*They get to their feet.*
MRS HIGSON *helpfully speaks to them.*

MRS HIGSON. Here you are. A number ten. You see, it's wrote up, on the front. That's right: on the *front*.

*But before she has finished her explanation they have gone to board it.*

*Garnish's private office.*
GARNISH, *wearing hat and overcoat, is standing at his desk, pulling papers out of his brief-case – not only papers, a pair of pyjamas and a toilet-case come out as well – and replacing them by others. He is obviously in a great hurry.*
PETER *is in attendance, awaiting instructions.*

GARNISH. Thank God that was the last sight of Paris I've got to suffer this month. Now look, very quickly, before I go out again: I've just been into the Town Planning on my way from the airport . . . there's a new spot of trouble about the Consort Street demolitions. You'll have to alter the schedule, so that all they touch this first week is the shops and nothing else. It's not too late, is it? Right. (*He buzzes on the intercom.*) Miss Waters, I'm back from Paris; I'm off to lunch at the club in precisely thirty seconds. (*He turns away from the intercom to throw a question at* PETER.) What's happened to Krank? (*The telephone rings. He answers it.*) Just a moment. Hello . . . Speaking . . . Good morning, Sir Harold . . . There was fog at Le Bourget. I'm on my way now; I'll bring all the documents . . . yes, what was that? (*His other phone rings.*) Hell's bells and buckets of . . . (*He answers it.*) Garnish; hello? . . . Oh, Mr Treddlehoyle? Can you wait a moment, Jim, I'm on the other line . . . (*To* SIR HAROLD.) I may as well warn you in advance, Sir Harold, I've got a proposal worked out for some sort of compromise, which I hope will meet *your* approval: I can't vouch for the Archdeacon. (*To* TREDDLEHOYLE, *whose voice is burbling in the receiver*.) Look, Jim, please be reasonable: I'm *occupied* at this moment . . . (*To* SIR HAROLD.) Very well, Sir Harold, I'll be along in five minutes. Goodbye. (*He rings off the first phone, and talks to* TREDDLEHOYLE.) I'm sorry, Jim, it'll have to wait. I'm very very busy. I'm just going out; you must ring me tomorrow – good-bye. (RUTH *has entered and is standing waiting. He sees her*.) Yes? What's the matter?

RUTH. Can I see you a moment, Mr Garnish . . . it's about Intake Road. I . . .

GARNISH. No, no, not now, I haven't got time. (*He realizes that he has not yet rung off* TREDDLEHOYLE'S *line: the voice is still burbling. He speaks rather rudely into the instrument*.) Jim, I said good-bye. I'm sorry, lad, but I mean it. (*He rings off*.) Peter, you know what you're doing? And while you're at it, find out from Krank about the state of his City Hall Canteen. It's quite a possibility that that chap isn't going to be working here much longer. So you'll have to take over whatever he's on. Ruth, you can help him . . . If anybody wants me, I shall be at the club. I *hope* we're going to sort out this Cathedral nonsense at last. I *don't* want to be interrupted: but of course, if any emergency . . . All right – good-bye.

*He rushes out with his brief-case.*

RUTH. Krank's got the sack!

PETER. I'd not be surprised. Can you honestly tell me he hasn't been asking for it?

RUTH. Yes, but even so . . .

PETER. Completely irresponsible. I happen to know he's made a terrible mess of that job at the City Hall. The fact is, with these aliens, they think they know the lot: but they've no application, they've no sense of loyalty. I wouldn't give 'em house-room. You know, really, I wouldn't . . .

*Dining-room of a businessmen's club.*

*A corner of the dining-room, with one table in an alcove. The style of decoration is ponderous, with a good deal of heavy oak Tudorish panelling. Some civic and other coats of arms on the walls, and prints showing views of the city in the nineteenth century. The table has seats for three. The two outside ones are occupied by* SIR HAROLD SWEETMAN *and the* ARCHDEACON. *They are eating.* SWEETMAN *is large and slow, with very sharp, shrewd eyes. The* ARCHDEACON *is handsome, healthy and not noticeably spiritual.* GARNISH *rushes in, full of apologies, hangs up his coat and hat on a peg behind the table, sticks his brief-case on the floor, and sits between them.*

GARNISH. I'm sorry, I'm sorry: I'm late! Thick fog at Le Bourget. Sir Harold, Archdeacon, how d'ye do! (*To the* WAITER.) I'll have the usual, please, Jack. Right. Now then. Does anybody object if we come downright down to it and face up directly to these unfortunate differences? Good. Archdeacon, you've had your architect's report on the fabric of the Lady Chapel, which I have been studying in the plane, as a matter of fact. Perhaps, though, for the benefit of Sir Harold Sweetman, you wouldn't mind giving us the gist?

*The* WAITER *hovers with the wine list.*

Ah, I think a bottle of that one, please, and the Sauterne, number 72, to go with the Archdeacon's fish.

*The* WAITER *goes.*

ARCHDEACON. Sir Harold, this report has been causing us very grave concern. A crack has appeared in the south wall immediately to the west of the sedilia: it already runs at least twenty feet!

(*The* WAITER *brings* GARNISH'S *food and then the bottles of wine.*)

We are advised, furthermore, that any continued extension of the crack is bound to affect the stonework of the fan-vault – fifteenth century, Sir Harold, and justly celebrated throughout Europe – Mr Garnish, I am quite sure, knows all about *that*.

GARNISH. Let me make this perfectly clear, Archdeacon: as a practising architect, the last thing I want to see is damage or decay to the structure of a cathedral. Sir Harold, I know, will be in complete agreement with me there. Now, here is the crucial point: what are your grounds for claiming that our excavations across the road are responsible ? The fifteenth century, y'know, was a long, long time ago – oh it *was !* . . . and buildings deteriorate with age, just the same as you or I do.

ARCHDEACON. It is naturally difficult to prove . . .

GARNISH. Aha!

ARCHDEACON. But our architect considers that the balance of probability . . .

GARNISH. No, sir, it won't do! You won't stand that up in a court of law. I'm sorry, but you won't! Now, look here, Archdeacon: I am going to lay out a compromise – with, I hope, Sir Harold Sweetman's tacit approval. We admit nothing. But in view of the beauty of the ancient building and its historic place in the life of this city, we are prepared to incorporate into the structure of the Quicksnack Breakfast Food Offices a ferro-concrete reinforcing raft, to extend from our basement story, beneath the surface of the road, and tying back under your Lady Chapel foundations, thereby securing them against any further subsidence. (*He brings up his brief-case and takes out a drawing, which he hands to the* ARCH-DEACON.) Here is a rough sketch of what my engineer has in mind. All paid for by Quicksnack, but leaving you to meet the cost of repairs to the Cathedral itself: because we admit no liability. Now then, what do you say, Sir Harold?

SWEETMAN. Yes. You mustn't imagine, Archdeacon, that what is sometimes called Big Business is not fully alive to the necessary values of our national heritage.

ARCHDEACON (*pondering the drawing*). Ye-es . . . It certainly seems a most generous offer. But we *were* rather hoping I could persuade you to agree to stop all further work on the site, at least temporarily, until . . .

*The* WAITER *has come and is whispering to* GARNISH.

GARNISH (*to the* WAITER). What's that? Who? No no no, I can't possibly see him now. Ask him to wait. (*He turns back to the* ARCHDEACON *as the* WAITER *goes.*) You do appreciate, Archdeacon, that the amount of money involved in this contract makes that a pretty impracticable suggestion. Sir Harold?

SWEETMAN. Yes. Emphatically, yes.

*The* WAITER *is again whispering, in agitation, into* GARNISH'S *ear.*

GARNISH. What's the matter? No! . . . Where is he?

*The* WAITER *gestures helplessly in the direction of the entrance, as* TREDDLEHOYLE *is heard calling, off.*

TREDDLEHOYLE. Mr Garnish! Mr Garnish!

GARNISH. Excuse me, I'll deal with it . . . (*He gets up hurriedly and meets* TREDDLEHOYLE, *who is hastening towards him, flushed and furious.*) Jim, didn't the waiter tell you? I'm very busy indeed; this is very important. I can't leave these gentlemen now . . .

TREDDLEHOYLE. You've been putting me off for the past seven days . . .

GARNISH. Past seven days? What are you talking about – I've been in Paris! Look, will you wait for me at the bar? I'll be with you in twenty minutes – I'll get them to give you a drink – waiter!

TREDDLEHOYLE (*raising his voice*). No! I won't have it! I won't have you setting me wi' the milk bottles in the back-yard while you're out front on your tennis-lawn supping tea with the Archbishop. (*He is suddenly aware of the embarrassment of the party, but by no means cowed.*) If I'm causing offence, gentlemen, I'll apologize in advance, but I've been trying to see Mr Garnish for over a week and it's costing me four thousand pounds!

GARNISH. How could I possibly see you, Jim? I tell you I've been in Paris.

TREDDLEHOYLE. I know too damn well you've been in Paris: and I'm not going to ask you neither, with a clergyman here, what you've been *doing* there!

SWEETMAN *and the* ARCHDEACON *are obviously annoyed.*

GARNISH. Jim, this is: Sir Harold Sweetman: Archdeacon Pole-Hatchet. We were discussing the crack in the Cathedral wall that the Archdeacon believes has been caused by our work in progress across the road for Sir Harold's new office-block. As you will appreciate, it is rather a delicate question.

TREDDLEHOYLE. Oh . . . Aye, well, I suppose that it must be.

*A pause. Then the* ARCHDEACON *suddenly gets to his feet with angry decision.*

ARCHDEACON. A delicate question, gentlemen, that still has to be resolved. I am sorry, but unless you can undertake . . .

GARNISH. Archdeacon, you're not leaving us!

ARCHDEACON (*cold and implacable*). I am afraid I shall have to. Choral evensong is at three o'clock this afternoon.

GARNISH. But you haven't had your sweet!

ARCHDEACON. I have made an excellent luncheon, Mr

Garnish, thank you. This matter of a concrete reinforcement: I will naturally refer it to our own architect for an opinion: but I am afraid that your repeated refusal to suspend site operations leaves me with no alternative but to instruct our legal advisers to apply to the Courts for an injunction. A step I had wished to avoid.

SWEETMAN. Archdeacon, if you please – will you not sit down again? I am quite sure that all this can be amicably talked over. Yes.

ARCHDEACON. No, sir, I think not. Present circumstances perhaps are hardly propitious. Good afternoon, Sir Harold, Mr Garnish. I will leave you in peace to your various businesses – big, and otherwise . . .

*He goes.*

SWEETMAN. Not a very satisfactory meeting, Mr Garnish. I should have preferred to compromise. I am not fond of litigation. Well, I, too, must be on my way. I have a great deal to attend to.

GARNISH. Then, when am I going to see you again, sir? Perhaps we can have a word at the Lord Mayor's reception on Wednesday – if you're going to be there?

SWEETMAN. I think it unlikely. Good afternoon. Good afternoon, Mr er . . .

*He, too, goes.* GARNISH *bangs the table with frustration.*

GARNISH. Oh – it's a bit late ordering lunch now, but I dare say they could still bring you summat. What would you care for? The Archdeacon had *fish!*

TREDDLEHOYLE. No. No, I won't eat, thank you very much. I've fair dropped you into it, haven't I, Gilbert?

GARNISH (*grinding his teeth*). Sweetman was my biggest client. I'll lay you my black Bentley to your errand-boy's push-bike that when he builds his new oatcake factory at the beginning of next year he gets another man to do it. And I was as certain of that job as I wear pants on my backside.

(*The* WAITER *is hovering with the menu.*)

Two whiskies – big ones. And don't you grin at me, Jack: I'm not in that sort of mood. Right?

(*The* WAITER *goes.*)

Now then, what's all this nonsense about four thousand pounds?

TREDDLEHOYLE. You may very well call it nonsense when you're stuck into your beefsteak with Amalgamated Corn and the High Church of England. But it's not nonsense to me Gilbert Garnish – it's my life's blood: and I can tell you I take no pleasure in watching it run away. Let alone the other troubles: I'm talking about my roof.

GARNISH. What's the matter with your roof?

TREDDLEHOYLE. You don't even know. Every timber of that roof's got to come off and go on again and you call yourself my architect and you don't even *know* about it!

*The* WAITER *brings the drinks.*

GARNISH. Steady, steady, lad. Thank you very much, Jack. Now, you drink this down you and tell me what it's all about. But try and tell me *quietly*, with a bit of control. There's other folk in this dining-room. We don't want it all round the world. (TREDDLEHOYLE *drinks.*) That's right. Now take a deep breath and tell me . . .

*Treddlehoyle's fish shop: the office.*
*One of the walls has been half broken down, so that we can see through to* WORKMEN *busy in the wet-fish department.* KRANK *is talking to* DORIS.

DORIS. Well, I'm sure I don't know what to say. You can't

expect me to discuss this sort of business without Mr Treddlehoyle here. It's not right to ask me.

KRANK. Oh now, gracious lady, you do yourself a disservice with such modesty. Yes, indeed, you do: because I *know*, because in the eyes of a wife I can read it, where is the spirit and the strength of her house.

DORIS. You're not at Scarborough now, you know, propping up the door of an hotel bedroom.

KRANK (*left a little behind by that one*). Hotel bedroom? Scarborough? Dear lady, I hope I *never shall* be . . . Listen: there is absolutely no doubt that your husband is going to have to pay two or three thousand pounds additional to what he expected, because of this unfortunate business of the roof.

DORIS. We'll be practically bankrupt! He's spent twenty-five years building up this business.

KRANK. Here is my offer. As you know, I am the landlord of next door and next door. I would like to buy yours as well and obtain an economical building unit.

DORIS. But what would *we* do?

KRANK. You would pay me rent for the ground-floor shop. And for the upper floor – which you only use, do you not, for storage space and the like? I have a plan for conversion into what we call flatlets.

DORIS. But we need the space . . .

KRANK. You do? Oh, I don't know . . . something can be arranged, h'm? I assure you, gracious lady, I am a most accommodating landlord.

DORIS. You've got very accommodating manners, any road . . . How much?

KRANK. Two thousand pounds. And you yourself pay for whatever alterations have *already* been carried out by Durable Construction. They continue their work and I pay for the rest. I think we may have to cut down a little on some of the specification. I would prefer to take it into my own hands from those of Mr Garnish: but that can be settled.

DORIS. I think I'd better mash you a good pot of tea.

*He takes off his spectacles.*

*Garnish's private office.*

*Drawings and documents spread out on the desk and drawing-board. Gathered round are* GARNISH, TREDDLEHOYLE, PERKINS *and* RUTH.

GARNISH. There seems to be no question but we've been very unfortunate indeed. In fact, I'd go further; I'd say we'd been given the real mucky end of the shovel over this and that's no exaggeration.

TREDDLEHOYLE. *We've* been given it, eh?

GARNISH (*sharply*). Yes, I said *we*. Don't you go thinking this doesn't affect me, you know. My duty's to my client: and if my client's not satisfied, it means I'm a failure. You *do* recognize, don't you, that a rotten roof's a rotten roof, and if we hadn't discovered it now, in another two or three years – well, it'd *treble* your costs of replacement. I should think, if we're careful, Mr Perkins's estimate of the present increase can probably be brought down by a couple of hundred, but . . .

TREDDLEHOYLE. But what about the other? All these damn great extras it seems I've got to pay! That lavatory concrete alone, and then eighty-eight quid for shifting one little drainpipe under the floor!

GARNISH (*very startled*). Eighty-eight quid!

*He swings round to* RUTH.

RUTH. Well, you see, the position of the gully, and then the brickwork of the pier, and then there was the original foundations and . . .

GARNISH. Who made the Variation Orders? You?

RUTH. What else could I do? You were always in Paris!

PERKINS. It was all perfectly regular, Mr Garnish. I *did* think it excessive: but Mr Treddlehoyle had signed his approval.

TREDDLEHOYLE. Of course I signed for it! *I* didn't know how much it wor going to cost. I just got these letters, like from your secretary. Naturally I took it you knew what you wor at!

GARNISH (*perspiring*). Let me see the letters. (*He ruffles through a handful of letters, his brow growing blacker at each one. He thrusts the papers at* RUTH'S *face.*) Do you mean to say you authorized all *this*?

RUTH. Why, yes, I . . .

GARNISH (*beating the top letter with an angry hand*). Three and a half inches of *screed* all over the lavatory! Have you gone off your nut, girl?

RUTH. But the fall towards the gully . . .

GARNISH. The fall towards the gully! I *told* you, if you had any difficulties to ask Peter Appleyard. *Did* you ask him?

RUTH. Well . . .

GARNISH. Yes or no?

RUTH. No. You see, I . . .

GARNISH. Get out, get back to the drawing-office. Tell Peter to find you some nice little corner of Consort Street to fiddle around with, where you can't do any damage. I thought I could trust you, but it seems I was wrong.

RUTH. I'm very sorry, Mr Garnish. I really didn't mean . . .

GARNISH. Go on, clear away . . . All right, Mr Perkins: I don't think we need trouble you any more. Extremely good of you to look in at such very short notice.

RUTH *goes out.*

PERKINS. Good afternoon, Mr Garnish.
GARNISH. Good afternoon.

(PERKINS *goes out.*)

Now, don't you be worried about the eighty-eight quid,

Jim. You can take it off my fee. I can't think what she was playing at . . . Let's have another look at this confounded roof.

TREDDLEHOYLE. I don't give a damn for the roof. I'm prepared to accept your word it couldn't be avoided. Though it strikes me, like, somebody *might* have borne it in mind from the very beginning . . . You see, what's getting at me is when I brought this job to you, you gave me to understand you wor going to do it yourself.

GARNISH. But I *have* been . . .

TREDDLEHOYLE. You *have* been. You mean you didn't turn it over to none of your smart partners. 'Stead of which, you give it to a gormless young chicken what's hardly left hold of the old hen's back feathers!

GARNISH. Look, you've got to appreciate the way these big offices work. Ruth Parsons is fully qualified . . .

TREDDLEHOYLE. Qualified for what? Ruining my business?

*The telephone rings.* GARNISH *answers it.*

GARNISH. Just a minute . . . Hello . . . Gilbert Garnish . . . Yes, he's with me. I'll give him the phone. It's your missus: she says it's urgent.

*He hands the phone to* TREDDLEHOYLE.

TREDDLEHOYLE. Hello? Doris? What's happened? . . . Eh, you don't say . . . Go on, love: let's have all the figures. I'm very glad you rang . . .

*Garnish's drawing-office.*
*All at their boards except* KRANK.
PETER *and* LESLIE *are working,* RUTH *is staring at her drawing with a miserable expression.*
*The door opens and* KRANK *slides in in his usual manner and goes through his usual business with holdall and street clothes.*
PETER *and* LESLIE *look up as he enters.*

PETER. Here he is, the man himself.

LESLIE. Some say 'Good old Krank', but others tell the truth.

PETER. We all thought you'd left us.

KRANK. Me? Left you? Oh, my goodness no. What an idea . . . Have there been any telephone calls?

PETER. There have not.

KRANK. Oh . . . a pity . . . (*He sees* RUTH *and walks over to her, to talk to her in a whisper.*) Hello, Ruth. You do not appear to be too happy. What is the matter?

RUTH. Nothing.

KRANK. No? . . . Here is a secret: what Peter says just now, that he thought I had left – it is nearly the truth. You see, I *may* be leaving: very soon. I would like you to come with me and to live with me. Will you?

RUTH (*startled into a sudden reaction*). No, I won't. Why should I?

KRANK (*easily*). There is to be no compulsion. Only I just thought . . .

RUTH (*sharply*). Live with you for how long?

KRANK (*easily*). It is not always possible to plan my life very far in advance. Should we say, a month or two? And then . . .

RUTH (*not without humour, but angry notwithstanding*). That's just you all over. And who takes my place after that? Mrs Treddlehoyle, I suppose.

*Enter* GARNISH, *furious: followed by* TREDDLEHOYLE.

GARNISH. Where's that man Krank!

KRANK. Mr Garnish?

GARNISH. Oh, you're *in* for a change, are you? Now listen to me: have you been going behind my back with offers for Mr Treddlehoyle's property?

KRANK. A small proposition. It occurred to me that . . .

GARNISH (*pointing him out to* TREDDLEHOYLE). Here he is. Look at him. He's a crooked little spiv. You'll be interested to know, Krank, that the police have been asking me a few questions about your doings.

KRANK. Questions are nothing. *Proof* is the essential.

GARNISH (*to* TREDDLEHOYLE). Well: if you want to take his offer, you're welcome and be damned. You can have him as your architect: you can have him as your landlord. I dare say he'll bloom just as gorgeous in either situation.

TREDDLEHOYLE (*slowly*). My good lady was very impressed by Mr Krank's proposals. I've got half a mind to accept them, young man. And while we're on about it, you can give me again what I've always been used to: that's an open-fronted shop where me customers can come and they can see what they're buying. It's real downright daft to have all them snobby glass windows for the sort of trade we carry. I want an architect as understands my business . . . And let me tell you, Gilbert Garnish, I've owned me own fish shop since the day me old dad died. I never dreamt the time would come when I'd find it an economy to be another man's tenant.

GARNISH. If you really feel you've got to sell out, for Heaven's sake let *me* handle it. Why, I'd as soon turn you over to the public hangman as a little creeper like this! Now listen: Prince Consort Street. We're building twenty new shops – Leslie, get the drawing . . . it's a grand speculation: I could put your name down for one now . . . (*He takes the drawing that* LESLIE *brings over.*) Here, look at this . . .

TREDDLEHOYLE. No. It's no good. It's not worth my while to listen to you any longer. I thought I could ha' trusted *you* to do me a good job.

GARNISH. But, Jim, all o' these things could have gone wrong with anybody.

TREDDLEHOYLE. Oh aye, they could. I'll not deny that. But I still can't get over that you don't understand why when a man says he'll do work for me I expect him to do it. Aye, aye, you wor in Paris. Well, I don't work in Paris. *I* work in

the Intake Road, and it's Friday afternoon – I've a lot of
fish to sell. So I'm off back to sell it. Mr Krank, if you'd
care to come round this evening, you and I might have a
talk. Good afternoon, Gilbert.

*He goes out.*
GARNISH *runs after him and calls.*

GARNISH. Hey, Jim, wait on a minute . . . Jim . . .
(*But* TREDDLEHOYLE *is gone.* GARNISH *comes back into the
room.*
KRANK *starts quietly putting all his goods into his holdall and
himself into his coat and hat.*)
Leslie, will you find out how many of the Consort Street
shops are still lacking a tenant, and then let me know. I dare
say we'll be able to fix him up with summat. (*His eye falls
on* KRANK.) I don't want to see *you* ever again.

KRANK *smiles, salutes, and slips out of the office. As he goes
past* RUTH *he drops a key on her board and whispers.*

KRANK. I shall expect my supper at half past six o'clock . . .
Spaghetti Bolognese – O.K. ?
GARNISH. All these old chaps, they can't seem to appreciate
how the world works . . . Oh well, we'd better send him a
nice letter: and butter him up a bit, I suppose. All he really
wants, you know, is someone to sit by him and hold his hand
for a while . . . Peter, how's that bus station ? Have the
asphalters arrived yet ?
PETER. They should have come yesterday, but I don't think
they have.
GARNISH. Then get on to Barker and ask him why not! They're
*not* a good firm, I *shan't* use them again: they've *no* reliability, *no* loyalty to the job. Nowt but make-do-and-mend
and scrabble for the leavings. It's ridiculous giving them all
these contracts one after the other . . . All right, get on
with it . . .

# When is a Door not a Door?

*An Industrial Episode*

1958

WHEN IS A DOOR NOT A DOOR? was first produced at the Embassy Theatre, Swiss Cottage by the Central School of Drama on 2 June 1958 with the following cast:

| | | |
|---|---|---|
| MR HENDERSON, Managing Director | | Bernard Dandridge |
| MR GOLDSWORTH | } of the Office Staff | Nicholas Simons |
| MR GURNEY | | Graham Heppel |
| MR STOBO, a Trade Union Official | | Jeremy Kemp |
| FIRST WORKMAN | } Carpenters | John Scarborough |
| SECOND WORKMAN | | Giles Phibbs |
| MISS BROACH, Packing Shop Manageress | | Helen Willett |
| SALLY, Mr Henderson's Secretary | | Eva Huszar |
| TEA-GIRL | | Clare Stewart |
| FIRST WORKING GIRL | } of the Packing Shop | Shuna Black |
| SECOND WORKING GIRL | | Joan Clevedon |

Directed by Robert Cartland

The Scene is a factory, in England. The office of the Managing Director's Secretary; between the Managing Director's office and the office corridor.

The time is the Present, about ten o'clock in the morning.

# Notes for Production

*Characters:*

HENDERSON. He is youngish, brisk, intolerant and high-voiced. Very energetic.

GOLDSWORTH. Middle-aged, very serious, pompous; and rather slow.

GURNEY. An ex-officer type, and incompetent.

STOBO. Pushful and aggressive, but good-humoured.

FIRST WORKMAN. In the prime of life. With strong opinions.

SECOND WORKMAN. A young man, fairly respectful towards FIRST WORKMAN.

MISS BROACH. Of a certain age. Easily offended and generally harassed.

SALLY. A pretty girl in early twenties.

TEA-GIRL. Same age as SALLY, but a few social strata below.

WORKING GIRLS. Tough good-humoured young women, with some strength of character.

*General Notes:*

The two WORKMEN do not take any notice of the conversation and actions of the others, except where indicated in the text. They may now and then look up, but without any apparent interest or comprehension of the events taking place. Their work upon the door should be carried out completely realistically, and should be rehearsed so as to terminate properly where the stage directions say. The job should be seen to be properly done before they leave the stage. The scenery need not be more than sketched into place: but the door and door-frame between the outer office and the corridor should be real.

*The scene is divided in the middle by a partition. One side repre-
sents a corridor, and the other side an office. In the rear wall of
the office is a door marked 'Managing Director'. In the partition
is a door, standing ajar, marked 'Managing Director's Secretary'.
In the Office* SALLY *sits typing at a desk, upon which is an inter-
office speaking installation.* TWO WORKMEN, *carrying a heavy
toolbag, come along the corridor and stop outside the door.*

FIRST WORKMAN (*studying a piece of paper*). Well, here we
are. 'Doorway between outer office and corridor.' Outer
office: right? Corridor? Right.

SECOND WORKMAN. Right.

FIRST WORKMAN. It says: it won't hold shut. Let's have a
see. (*He tests the door by opening and shutting it several times.
Seeing* SALLY, *he nods casually.*) Morning.

SALLY. Good morning.

SECOND WORKMAN (*to* FIRST WORKMAN). It's warped, see.
Sticks in the frame. (*He tests the door also.*) Take it out,
won't we?

FIRST WORKMAN. Right.

*They stand back in the corridor and study the door.*

SALLY. Do you know that door's been jamming since before
the Christmas holiday. It's dreadful. I've had to stay all of
last Saturday in bed with a stiff neck. So I told Mr Henderson. I mean, if nobody else . . .

SECOND WORKMAN (*to* FIRST WORKMAN). Top or bottom?

FIRST WORKMAN. Top corner. Take it off with the plane.
Eighth inch. Quarter inch. Should do.

SECOND WORKMAN. Nothing to it, really.

FIRST WORKMAN (*sucks his teeth*).

HENDERSON *comes briskly down the corridor and strides past
them into the outer office.*

HENDERSON. Good morning, Miss Nuttall.

SALLY. Good morning, Mr Henderson. (*She indicates the* WORKMEN.) Oh, Mr Henderson, the door . . .

HENDERSON (*impatiently*). So I see. So I see. Mr Gurney in this morning?

SALLY. I think so, Mr Henderson.

HENDERSON. Buzz for him, will you? I want him *now*.

*He goes into his office and slams the door.*

SALLY (*buzzing the desk-speaker*). Mr Gurney? Mr Henderson's just asking for you, sir . . . Yes sir. (*She clicks the button to transfer the line.*) Mr Gurney's on his way, Mr Henderson.

*She clicks off, and returns to her typing: which she continues intermittently throughout the play.*

FIRST WORKMAN. The little driver ought to do it. (*The* SECOND WORKMAN *hands him a small screwdriver from the bag.*) Right. (*He starts to unscrew the hinges of the door.*) Just hold her up so she don't fall out as I unscrew, will you . . . Hoo ah: stiff devil, this one . . . ah!

GURNEY *comes hurrying down the corridor and goes straight through into the outer office.*

GURNEY. Morning, Sally: how's the love-life?

SALLY (*chillingly*). Please, Mr Gurney. I think you're wanted urgently.

GURNEY (*disconcerted*). Oh. Oho. Is he waiting?

SALLY. Of course, Mr Gurney.

GURNEY. God save us. What's he after now? What's the racket this morning, hey?

SALLY (*chillingly*). I really couldn't say, Mr Gurney. I'm sorry. You'd better walk straight through: he's waiting.

GURNEY *knocks at the inner door and opens it.*

GURNEY. Morning, F.H., what's the panic?

*He goes in and shuts the door behind him.*

FIRST WORKMAN. Now hold her steady while I take these lads at the bottom out. (*The* SECOND WORKMAN *is supporting the leaf of the door as the hinges are unscrewed.*) Right. All scroffed up with paint, these . . . You see, it's what I say all the time. It's apathy. Well, look at it. Apathy. I mean, take Russia.

SECOND WORKMAN. What's Russia got to do with it?

FIRST WORKMAN (*disgusted*). That's what I mean, then . . . You stand there: and you ask me what's Russia got to do with it. If it wasn't for your apathy, you'd know.

SECOND WORKMAN. Oh, draw it mild, mate . . .

FIRST WORKMAN (*scornfully*). 'Draw it mild, mate, draw it mild' – You're no better than *he* is, 'cept you put it in different words.

SECOND WORKMAN. Better than who is?

FIRST WORKMAN (*jerking his thumb towards the inner office*). Him. 'Morning, Sally: how's the love-life?' I mean – 'scuse me, miss – I mean, listen to it.

SECOND WORKMAN. Oh, *him*. They all talk like that, these fellers. It's the way they learn 'em, y'know. 'Course, they get paid for it according.

FIRST WORKMAN. What you gain on the swings, you lost it on the hoop-la . . . O.K. O.K. Let's lift her away. (*They lift the door out of its frame, backing with it into the office.*) Careful, steady, *to* you.

SECOND WORKMAN. 'Scuse us, miss: we'll take it in the corridor, eh? (*They carry the door out of the office.*) *To* you. Steady.

FIRST WORKMAN. Careful.

SECOND WORKMAN. Steady.

FIRST WORKMAN. Down.

*The door is set down against the wall.*

SECOND WORKMAN. Well, there we are. Have a drag?

FIRST WORKMAN. Don't mind. Ta.

*They light a pair of half-smoked cigarettes, and stand easy.
The desk-speaker buzzes.*

SALLY (*answering it*). Hello, Mr Henderson's secretary. Can I
help you? . . . Oh, Miss Broach. Yes . . . Good gracious
me . . . But he'll be furious. Oooh . . . Oh dear, oh dear,
and on a Monday morning, too. It just seems everything's
to happen on a Monday, and just after the holidays, too, I
mean . . . Yes, Miss Broach, I'll get you through to him
directly. (*She clicks to transfer the line.*) Oh, Mr Henderson.
Miss Broach on the line. She says the girls in the Packing
Shop have stopped work, Mr Henderson . . . Yes . . .
Oh, I'll put her on directly, Mr Henderson. (*She clicks the
apparatus again.*) You're through to Mr Henderson, Miss
Broach.

*She clicks off.*

*The* TEA-GIRL *comes down the corridor, pushing a trolly
loaded with teapot and cups, etc.*

SECOND WORKMAN. Oi oi, tea's up.

TEA-GIRL (*passing him coldly*). You're not allowed to smoke
in the corridors.

SECOND WORKMAN. Who says?

*She goes into the outer office.*

TEA-GIRL. Tea-time, dear.

SALLY. One extra this morning, Doris, please. Mr Gurney's
in with Mr Henderson. I think . . .

TEA-GIRL. Looks a bit draughty here this morning.

GURNEY *comes out of the inner office.*

HENDERSON (*from within*). And tell him I'm not having it!
I want an answer by Wednesday, or I'll know the reason.

GURNEY *hastens away down the corridor.*

SALLY. Well, he *was* in with him, anyway.

*The* TEA-GIRL *pours out tea.*

TEA-GIRL. They're going on strike in the Packing Shop, did
you know, dear?

SALLY (*discreetly*). Well, yes, I did hear *something*.

TEA-GIRL. It's true. Imagine. Well, I mean, I'm not surprised.
It's that frozen in there this weather, I'd do it meself for
half the money. Why don't he put in radiators that *work*?
He can't expect . . .

HENDERSON (*appearing at the door*). Miss Nuttall!

*He goes in again.*

SALLY. Coming, Mr Henderson. Oh lord, where's his sugar . . .

*She hunts around for the sugar and succeeds in upsetting her
own cup of tea.*

TEA-GIRL. Watch out!

SALLY (*furious*). Oh!

TEA-GIRL (*rather sulky*). Not my fault.

SALLY *goes into the inner office with a cup of tea, sugared, and
her notebook. The* TEA-GIRL *mops up the spill, clucking with
annoyance.*

FIRST WORKMAN (*selecting a plane from his toolbag*). You see,
the trouble is: I've always said it: it's not rightly a question
whether they're right or whether they're wrong. It's the
basic *impressions* that count. And don't tell me no different.
Basic. Now take Suez.

SECOND WORKMAN. You take it.

FIRST WORKMAN (*beginning to plane the edge of the door*).
Well, what happens? He says: it's lah de dah this, and it's
lah de dah that, and play the game, Britons, play the game.

And what does Nasser do? He walks in, *don't he?* He nicks the old canal. And wouldn't you? He's a smart man, Nasser, he knows the Old School Tie when he sees it. 'You play the game, me boys, and I play dirty.' That's what *he* says.

SECOND WORKMAN. Huh. And what about Eden's free holiday at Bermudas, eh? What about *that?* After all that shambles. Just like, in'it?

FIRST WORKMAN. Look, you go back to the yard this afternoon. You tell our boss: 'Look here, boss, you said go and see to that doorway, it's jamming. We gone and done the window by mistake: what are we to do?' And what does he say to that? He says: 'All *right*, my lad, don't you worry, my lad, all you done, boy, is make an error of judgement. Anyone could do it. So take yourself a week at Brighton and credit it to the firm.' It's likely, *in'it?* Bleedin' likely.

*The* TEA-GIRL *wheels her trolly out again into the corridor.*

SECOND WORKMAN (*intercepting her*). Here, lovey, let's have a cuppa . . .

TEA-GIRL (*tartly*). This is for the offices, this is. There's a canteen for *you*, across the yard.

GURNEY *comes back along the corridor.*

SECOND WORKMAN (*to* TEA-GIRL). Ah, who's to know . . .

GURNEY. Tea, tea, do I see tea!

*He rapidly pours himself out a cup and carries it into the outer office.*

SECOND WORKMAN (*still wheedling*). Come on now, just a quick one . . .

TEA-GIRL. I've got me cups counted. You leave them alone.

GOLDSWORTH *comes along the corridor.* GURNEY *enters the inner office.*

GOLDSWORTH (*to the* WORKMEN *in passing*). No smoking in the corridor, please.

GOLDSWORTH *enters the outer office as* SALLY *comes out of the inner office.*

TEA-GIRL (*triumphantly to the* WORKMEN). See.

*She wheels her trolly away.*

GOLDSWORTH (*to* SALLY). Is he in, Miss Nuttall?

SALLY. He's waiting for you, sir.

GOLDSWORTH *knocks and enters the inner office.* SALLY *sits to her table again and continues typing.* GURNEY *comes out of the inner office.*

GURNEY (*flustered*). Last week's packing schedules, Sally: where are they?

SALLY (*coldly*). In the General Office, Mr Gurney, where they always are. You'll have to ask Miss Hawkins.

GURNEY. Oh, blast and bloody . . . (*She looks at him, and he becomes more flustered.*) I *beg* your pardon. Yes, I'll ask Miss Hawkins. (*He goes out into the corridor, muttering as he passes the* WORKMEN.) There's a lot I'd like to ask Miss Hawkins. There's a lot I'd like to tell Miss Hawkins, Miss Hawkins . . .

*He goes out, cursing to himself.*

SECOND WORKMAN (*continuing the previous discussion*). Well, how do you account for it, then? I mean, Bermudas and that.

FIRST WORKMAN. Why, it's all the same; he plays their game, they give him a holiday. But as for anyone getting anything *done*, I mean *results* – oh ho ho no. Now see, take the Olympic Games.

MISS BROACH *enters along the corridor and goes into the outer office.*

MISS BROACH. Is Mr Henderson disengaged, Miss Nuttall?

SALLY. Mr Goldsworth's in with him, Miss Broach. Just a moment, I'll see . . . (*She clicks the desk-speaker.*) Mr Henderson, Miss Broach is here . . . Yes, Mr Henderson. (*She clicks off.*) He won't be a moment, Miss Broach . . . Is it going to be a proper strike, do you think?

MISS BROACH. How should *I* know, my dear?

SALLY. Well, what's it all about?

MISS BROACH. I'm only the Shop Manageress, my dear; I'm told nothing. Except one minute they're all at work, and the next minute they're all in the toilets laughing their heads off.

SALLY. What about?

FIRST WORKMAN. The Russians win the lot. I mean, by and large, they win 'em. Now why? It's 'cos of apathy. 'Cos there's no *passion*, that's why.

MISS BROACH. I'm sure I can't imagine, my dear. It's quite beyond *me*, I can tell you. It began with some nonsense about Dirty Money because of those gunmetal manifolds that had to be packed in grease, and then . . .

FIRST WORKMAN. What do they say to the English team before they go out on the field, eh?

SECOND WORKMAN. I dunno.

FIRST WORKMAN. Well, I'll tell you. It's 'Play the game, chaps, oh play the game. It doesn't matter who wins, only play the game.' But to these Russians – oh oh: 'You'll win the lot and you'll win bloody records; or there's cold breakfasts in Siberia . . .

GURNEY *re-enters along the corridor, carrying papers, and goes into the outer office.*

GURNEY. Ah, Miss Broach!

MISS BROACH. Good morning, Mr Gurney . . .

FIRST WORKMAN. . . . till Charlie Khrushchev tells you different!'

GURNEY (*savagely*). So the Packing Department's stuck its arm in up to the elbow again! As usual on a Monday.

MISS BROACH (*offended*). If we technical people had the proper co-operation from the office staff, there'd be no need at all for that sort of language, Mr Gurney.

GURNEY. And the best of luck!

*He enters the inner office.*

MISS BROACH. It's very well, very easy, to put the blame on me, but I don't control the wages policy, nor *yet* the annual holidays.

GOLDSWORTH *comes out of the inner office.*

GOLDSWORTH. Miss Broach, if you please.

GURNEY *comes out of the inner office.*

GURNEY. Just a moment, just a moment. Sally, F.H. is asking for . . .

HENDERSON (*from within*). Gurney!

GURNEY (*confused*). Yes, er – yes, F.H.?

HENDERSON (*from within*). Not the red one, you idiot, the blue!

GURNEY (*furiously to* SALLY). The blue one, the blue one – why can't you have these things ready? He's going to break my collarbone in a minute . . . Yes, there, you silly girl!

*He snatches a blue-covered file off her desk and goes in again.*

GOLDSWORTH. We'd better go in, Miss Broach.

MISS BROACH. Very well, Mr Goldsworth.

*He takes her into the inner office.*

FIRST WORKMAN (*completing the planing and standing up*). I think that ought to do it: what do you say? Just sand down the angle, and then we'll set her up again, then give a lick of paint. And Bob's your uncle. Hokey cokey.

SECOND WORKMAN (*looking in the toolbag*). We ain't got that much sanding left, you know. I thought you said there was some in the bag.

FIRST WORKMAN. Well, there is, in't there?

SECOND WORKMAN (*holds up a piece of sandpaper*). There's *this* piece. Like, rough, in't it? Not much, for us? I mean, there's none of the proper smooth.

FIRST WORKMAN (*vexed*). Ow.

SECOND WORKMAN. I thought you said there was some in the bag.

FIRST WORKMAN. That young lad said he'd put some in. He said it this morning. I'll sandpaper his backend for him, we get back at the yard. They're no better than a lot of Teds, these fellers.

SECOND WORKMAN. Ah, we'll make do with this. It's a botch, but it's a job.

FIRST WORKMAN. It's a botched job and that's *all* it is. You see what I'm telling you, you see what I'm telling you, there's no passion these days, there's no what I call a lust, it's a botch all round, six ways on the compass. Look at Hitler.

*He tests the edge of the door with a square, and begins sandpapering, carefully.*

STOBO *and two* WORKING GIRLS *come along the corridor and into the outer office.*

STOBO (*with an air of command*). Ha-h'm.

SALLY (*a little flustered*). Oh. Yes? Good morning.

STOBO. It's a deputation.

SALLY. Mr Henderson's in conference at the moment, I'm afraid.

STOBO. Tell him it's a deputation, Miss Nuttall. I've called these girls out and I'm here to tell him why.

FIRST GIRL. He knows why.

SALLY. Miss Broach is in with him, you know.

STOBO. That's neither here nor there. Miss Broach is Miss Broach. *We're* on about double rates for holiday shifts and we want the head-man.

SALLY. I'll see what I can do. (*She clicks the desk speaker.*) Mr

Henderson, there's Mr Stobo here from the Trade Union,
and some of the Packing Shop people in a deputation . . .
Yes, Mr Henderson. (*She clicks off, and repeats the answer,
nervously apologetic.*) He says: 'Stobo comes in and the rest
stay out,' Mr Stobo.

STOBO (*humorously*). All right: he's frightened for his life, is
he? You stay here, me dears: I'll call if I need help.

FIRST GIRL. Good luck, Harry boy.

SECOND GIRL. Tell 'em the tale.

*STOBO goes into the inner office.*

FIRST WORKMAN. He's a soldier. He's seen life. And more
than that. He's suffered. He was a corporal, see. Then they
put him in prison. I mean, he knows the force of strength,
doesn't he? I mean, like, you're Hitler: I'm Chamberlain.
So I come along with the old umbrella up, *crawling*: 'Oh
play the game, old boy, play the game.' Well what do you
do!

SECOND WORKMAN. I dunno. What do I do?

FIRST WORKMAN. You march into Poland! Stands to reason
you do. Come on, come on!

SECOND WORKMAN (*with a laugh*). Where, Poland?

FIRST WORKMAN. All right, laugh. But I've seen experience.
I know these things.

FIRST GIRL (*chatting to the SECOND GIRL as they wait*). I
said to him, 'Why not Butlins? We've never been, and it's
not expensive . . .'

SECOND GIRL. It *is*.

FIRST GIRL. We-ell. It couldn't be worse than that place in
Llandudno, three-and-six a day extra just 'cos we wanted a
bit of pork pie to our breakfasts. And Dad got his hernia
there.

SECOND GIRL. They didn't charge him for that, did they?

*Both GIRLS laugh.*

FIRST WORKMAN (*finishing the sandpapering*). O.K. . . . Let's take her in. (*They lift the door.*) Up, two. *To* you. Steady.

*They back into the outer office with it, squeezing the* GIRLS *against the wall.*

SECOND WORKMAN. Steady. 'Scuse us, love. *Up* yours, *down* mine. Steady.

*The door is held up in its frame again.*

FIRST WORKMAN. Right. I'll hold her this time, you screw.
SECOND GIRL (*laughs*).
FIRST WORKMAN (*to* SECOND GIRL). I'll tell your mother!

*He supports the door while the* SECOND WORKMAN *begins to refix the hinges.*
*High voices, unintelligible, are heard in the inner office.*
GURNEY *shoots out of the door.*

GURNEY (*passing the* WORKMEN). My God, don't let him catch you smoking! He'll burn my hair off!

*He hurries away along the corridor.*

FIRST GIRL. Sounds like Harry Stobo's bringing in the ceiling a little, don't it?
SECOND GIRL. Aha, he knows his strength, does Harry.

GOLDSWORTH *comes out of the inner office.*

GOLDSWORTH. Where's Mr Gurney?
SALLY. I don't know: he went off!
GOLDSWORTH (*harassed*). Oh dear . . .

*He goes in again.*

SECOND GIRL (*to* SALLY). Dunno why your mob don't do it.
SALLY. Do what?
SECOND GIRL. Well, same as us. Walk out on it. You don't tell me they serve *you* any better – worse, *I* know, 'cos we've

got the Union, all you got's your flannelling Staff Associa-
tion. That lot couldn't kick a donkey through a gate.

SALLY (*embarrassed*). I don't know, I'm sure . . . I've got to
do these letters.

HENDERSON (*within*). All very well, that's all very well . . .

STOBO (*within*). Mr Henderson . . .

HENDERSON (*within*). But that's not just money you're asking
for, you know . . .

STOBO (*within*). Mr Henderson . . .

GOLDSWORTH (*within*). On a wider front and a long-term
policy . . .

HENDERSON (*within*). It's not just a question of an extra six-
pence, you know, to buy lipstick for fifty silly girls: it's the
life-blood of this industry . . .

STOBO (*within*). Mr Henderson!

GOLDSWORTH (*within*). We have to consider the reactions not
only of the shareholders . . .

HENDERSON (*within*). Mr Goldsworth . . .

GOLDSWORTH (*within*). But also the Parliamentary Commis-
sion . . .

HENDERSON (*within: in a great bellow*). Mr Goldsworth, *I am
talking*!

*The noise from the inner office now drops suddenly.*

FIRST GIRL. Cor blimey.

SECOND WORKMAN. It's one thing talking. But passions,
lusts and that – hold her steady, mate, I'm not bang on the
hole here . . . O.K., O.K. – Passions, lusts: I mean, what
is it you want?

FIRST WORKMAN. What I'm *telling* you. It's everywhere
around these days; there's nothing matters, is there? You
want a bit of sense of truth of life, man. (*He starts to sing in
a melancholy tuneless fashion.*)

  'For life is hard and life is cruel
  And hits you where it hurts:

It's better to fight and die on your feet
Than fatten in the dirt.'
It's good philosophy, it is . . . What's the matter – can't
you manage the last two turns? Here: you need a *wrist* on
this job. (*He takes over the screwdriver and continues singing.*)
'I hid my money under the floor
Tied up in a woollen bag:
But the rats they came and ate it all
And left me never a rag.'

GURNEY *re-enters along the corridor, and goes into the outer
office.*

GURNEY (*to* SALLY). I can't find it anywhere – where is it,
where is it?

SALLY. I don't know what you're talking about, Mr Gurney,
I'm afraid. What's got into everybody this morning? It's
not a bit nice working here, and there's no use my pretend-
ing it is. If you can't remember your manners . . .

*Offstage office noise.*

GURNEY. Oh lord, oh lord . . . (*He turns on the* WORKING
GIRLS, *in a despairing appeal.*) Now honestly: is there any
real need at all?

SECOND GIRL. Need for what?

GURNEY. Oh, *you* know. I mean, there's Harry Stobo in there,
we all know, hitting F.H.'s desk for him and bellowing away
like a radioactive hairbrush, but . . .

HENDERSON (*within*). No no no . . .

FIRST GIRL. He's not the only one bellows, is he, Mr Gurney?

HENDERSON (*within*). It's no good, Stobo; it won't wash,
man, it won't wash . . .

SECOND GIRL (*satirically*). Ah, it's the old old agony; it's all
right; so long as we don't shout, everybody's happy.

FIRST GIRL. It's models of industrial co-ordination.

SECOND GIRL. It's managers-labour co-operation, class-con-
sciousness barriers broke down . . .

FIRST GIRL. A demi-bloddy-paradise, write it in the papers . . .

SECOND GIRL. Just for so long as *we* don't shout!

GURNEY (*a little overwhelmed by their outburst*). Now, wait a
minute . . .

FIRST GIRL (*aggressive*). Wait a minute, wait a minute; don't
you go telling us to wait a minute . . .

SECOND GIRL (*nearly dancing with scorn*). Lah de dah, lah de
dah, Boss Henderson's bloody dog, bow-wow . . .

FIRST GIRL. Doggy doggy, bow-wow, wow, wow-wow-wow!

SECOND GIRL. Down, y'devil, *down*!

> *They both laugh.*
> GOLDSWORTH *appears at the door of the inner office.*

GOLDSWORTH. Gurney! Where in earth have you been,
Gurney? Mr Henderson wants . . .

GURNEY. In two shakes!

> GURNEY *goes out down corridor.*

HENDERSON (*within*). No no no . . .

STOBO (*within*). No no no no, it's no good, Mr Henderson.
I'm not taking *that* . . .

HENDERSON (*within*). I don't give a damn what the blasted
woman says . . .

> MISS BROACH, *weeping, runs out of the inner office, and away
> down the corridor.*
> STOBO *appears at the door of the inner office.*

STOBO (*strongly*). Come on, girls, come on: there's no good
for us in this place, no! We're going out and we're staying
out – that's all the Packing Shop, Mr F.H., and you'll be
lucky if it's not the Bottling Line and the Gum-kibble Floor
as well!

FIRST GIRL. Transport and General ought to come out in sympathy.

STOBO. Well, they might at that. So you'll lose your lorry-men and the canal-hands, and all, and then where will your orders be! Come on, girls!

*GURNEY appears in the corridor, indecisively.*
*STOBO goes out down the corridor in a rage.*
*The GIRLS follow him, barking and laughing at GURNEY as they go.*
*GURNEY goes out again.*
*HENDERSON comes out of the inner office.*

HENDERSON. Miss Nuttall! Take a letter!

SALLY. Yes, Mr Henderson.

*She starts gathering up her notebook and pencil.*
*HENDERSON begins dictating without giving her a minute. As he talks, he goes back into the inner office, and SALLY follows him, desperately trying to take down his words.*

HENDERSON. To Amalgamated Iron Hooks Limited, for attention Mr Longhandle. Dear Sirs, We are in receipt of yours of etcetera etcetera – get the date off the relevant file – and have pleasure in confirming herewith our acceptance of your quotation for the supply and delivery of thirteen-gross pattern – pattern whatever it is – ah – those hooks we ordered, find out what they are, and complete as usual. Send a copy to Haskins and Judson . . . (GURNEY *enters down the corridor and into the outer office, as* HENDERSON *reappears at his door, which has remained open.*) Gurney, I thought I asked you to check last week's packing schedules.

GURNEY. Yes – ah yes, F.H. I've got the figures here, yes . . .

HENDERSON. Are they collated?

GURNEY (*taken aback*). Well, ah, not exactly . . .

HENDERSON. Then for God's sake collate them! If there's going to be a full-blown strike, how the devil am I expected

to handle it without full knowledge of our resources? Mr
Goldsworth, I've told you what I want you to do.

GOLDSWORTH. Yes, Mr Henderson. By lunch-time. Yes.

*He hurries industriously away, down the corridor.*

GURNEY (*fumbling*). O.K., F.H., right-ho, smart as lucifer,
right, right, at the double . . .

*He follows* GOLDSWORTH.

HENDERSON *re-enters his office and slams the door.*

*The* WORKMEN, *having fixed the hinges, are now examining
the effect of the contents of a pot of paint taken from the bag.
The* SECOND WORKMAN *has dabbed a small patch on the
edge of the door and they stand back and regard it.*

FIRST WORKMAN. That's not a bad match at all. What do you
think?

SECOND WORKMAN. It's a bit light, you know.

FIRST WORKMAN. It ought to dry down dark enough. You've
got the shine on it, you see, with it being wet. Anyway, your
door fits right, there's no question.

SECOND WORKMAN. Bit on the small side, maybe: you'll
get draughts.

FIRST WORKMAN. Ah, not to signify. 'Course, it might sing.

SECOND WORKMAN (*painting the door, where they have planed
it*). Sing?

FIRST WORKMAN. With the wind in it, like. Being warped,
and then trimmed. My old grandma's kitchen door used to
sing, something violent. Like a regular aeroplane. The
Sopwith Camel, we used to call it, when we was kids. Bzzz,
hmmm, bzzz! You'd have to wait for a windy day to test this
one, though.

(SALLY *comes out of the inner office and sits at her machine.*)

Excuse me, miss. We've done.

SALLY. Oh, thanks ever so much. What a relief to be able to

work with the door shut at last. Or work at all, if it comes
to that.

FIRST WORKMAN. 'Course, it might sing. If you've a windy
day in the east and it sings, give us a call at the yard and
we'll come and sort it. Morning to you.

*He goes out into the corridor.*

SALLY (*puzzled*). Sing?

SECOND WORKMAN. Yeah, sing. Give us a call, we'll sort it.
Morning.

*He, too, goes out into the corridor and shuts the door carefully
behind him. They pack all their equipment in the toolbag.*

SALLY (*as the door closes*). Good morning, I'm sure.

FIRST WORKMAN. You see, what I tell you. That's a nice girl,
but she's like the rest of 'em in a place like this. They're
walking dummies. They've no passion, they've no *heart* on
the job at all. Offices *or* the assembly-lines, it's the same
thing everywhere. All rush – no urgency . . . Don't let
'em catch you smoking here, mate . . . Apathy all over.

SECOND WORKMAN. The bigger the firm – the less the
initiative.

FIRST WORKMAN. No passion. Nothing. Ah, it needs a crafts-
man to feel an honest rage about the world. I mean, take
Khrushchev. He's been a collier, hasn't he? He's worked in
the pits, he's seen life: he's suffered. We-ell . . .

*As they are about to leave the stage they meet the TEA-GIRL
pushing her trolly. They go off, past her; one of them apparently
having pinched her bottom on the way.*

TEA-GIRL (*furiously*). Get aht of it!

SALLY, *typing furiously, makes a mistake, swears to herself,
tears out the paper, and starts again.*

SALLY. Oh, *Oh;* what a morning. I don't know *where* I am . . .

*(The desk-speaker buzzes. She answers it.)* Yes, Mr Henderson . . .

*The* TEA-GIRL *comes into the outer office.*

TEA-GIRL *(loudly)*. Empties!

SALLY *(angrily)*. Oh, shut up, Doris, I'm trying to hear Mr Henderson . . . Yes, Mr Henderson . . . Yes . . .

TEA-GIRL *(very surly)*. How many cups inside?

SALLY. Very well, Mr Henderson . . . How should I know? Go and see!

TEA-GIRL. *I* can't go in there; you know I can't.

SALLY. Yes, Mr Henderson. *(She clicks the desk-speaker off.)* Look, can't you just wait a minute, while I'm on to the boss, for goodness' sake? Yappity-yap . . . God's sake, here's your tea-cups, and . . . *(SALLY shoves her cup across the desk: it drops on the floor and breaks.)* Well, it serves you right.

TEA-GIRL *(furious)*. Here, who's going to pay for this? It's not going to be stopped out of *my* wages, I can tell you . . .

SALLY. Oh, shut up!

TEA-GIRL. You shut up yourself, you smarty stuck-up cat!

SALLY. Don't you talk to me, you – you – you little tart, you! This is *my* office, *mine*, how dare you . . .

*The desk-speaker has buzzed again, but they ignore it in their anger.*

HENDERSON *(from within)*. Miss Nuttall. Miss Nuttall! *Miss Nuttall!*

*The desk-speaker buzzes continuously.*

# Friday's Hiding

*An Experiment in the Laconic*

1965

by
MARGARETTA D'ARCY
and
JOHN ARDEN

# Authors' Notes

We were asked to write a 'play without words' – in fact, this little play does contain some spoken passages (indicated by italics), because it seemed impossible to establish the plot without them. If they can be eliminated in the action and replaced by sufficiently expressive mime, we would raise no objections; though probably the opening expository speeches should remain and the song at the end ought not to be omitted.

Rather than cramp the producer by writing a very precise series of stage directions we have preferred (not being by temperament as definitive as, say, Mr Beckett) to tell a story, and to indicate by variations in the typography the different stages of the narrative and the relative rhythms of the action.

We have not attempted to specify the stage set or properties required. These are left to the discretion and convenience of the company. We did, however, visualize a largely bare stage, with the divisions between indoors and out or fields and yard established as much as possible through the action. Certain skeletal features may be necessary – e.g. a chimney-piece and a window-frame for the kitchen, and a cupboard for Mr Balfour's cash. The various hedges, thickets, etc., may be supplied by means of mime alone, or perhaps by one or two stylized pieces of foliage which should be whisked off the stage as soon as possible as their purpose has been served. The hay-cock ought to be practicable, but if it can be pulled up into the flies when done with it will not cumber the stage area. Other props such as hoes and dungforks will need some trial and error, perhaps, before an adequate convention is established. It seems to us that there are three possible ways of dealing with these.

1. Real articles.
2. No props but mimed action.
3. Plain sticks which can be used as hoes, or forks or anything else the actor cares to make them.

We would prefer the third way, which might be extended to
other props, such as furniture, so that a series of light boxes
or stools could serve as chairs, tables, walls, or any other solid
objects, being moved about by the actors to suit the particular
episode they are playing.

The backcloth should not be realistic – nor should it be
painted in that crude Walt Disney style which now seems to
be common for pantomimes and variety theatres. We would
prefer something which would present to the audience a stylized
suggestion of agricultural life – perhaps a bird's-eye view of an
entire farm and its fields or a series of vignettes like a contemporary version of pictures from a medieval Book of Hours
showing labourers engaged in their seasonal occupation.

Which brings us to the general style and content of the play.
Although at first reading it may appear to be nothing more than
old-fashioned kitchen-comedy and clodhopping knockabout,
it is intended (beneath its farcical surface) to be an accurate
representation of certain features of modern country life. The
story itself is based upon characters and circumstances well
known to the authors, and in performance the actors should
not forget certain social conditions which – carried *ad absurdum*
– could give rise to the events portrayed. For instance, on many
small farms the labourers belong to no trade union and therefore are entirely dependent upon their employer for both the
quantity and regularity of their wages. Farmers, who have a
reputation for meanness, are not necessarily *essentially* un-
charitable people: but their resources – even today – seem so
much at the mercy of unexpected accidents of nature and in-
explicable falls in prices and so forth that the foolishness of
letting money go which could have been kept becomes ingrained
into their character. Thus it would be a serious error for the

actors playing Mr and Miss Balfour to portray the one as a miserable old skinflint and the other as a dried-up sour spinster. They should much rather be the rosy-cheeked bright-eyed toytown figures out of a child's picture-book of the countryside, and let the opposite elements in their personalities arise through the action. Miss Balfour in particular needs considerable care if her role is not to degenerate into sentimentality. Her assumption of the wedding dress is really nothing more than a sudden gush of fantasy arising from her unexpected seizure of the money, and when she takes it off at the end the implication should be not so much 'the poor woman has lost her last chance of happiness', but rather 'of course the farmer's sister would never have been so daft as to marry a hired man'. Her status *vis-à-vis* the labourers is always one of superiority, even though they are driven into a sort of alliance by the 'closeness' of her brother. The play in sum is an ironic statement – *not* an affirmation – of the deep-rootedness of conservative values. It is also (and this is why we thought the subject suitable for mime) an exposition of the physical movements imposed by their occupation upon agricultural workers and the pleasure to be obtained from watching these. If this preface seems over-solemn it is only because we are anxious that the actors should base their performance upon a sound understanding of the lives of the characters they are to represent.

We have not had the opportunity of seeing this play either in rehearsal or performance: but our subsequent experience with a later piece (*The Royal Pardon*) has suggested to us the desirability of a musical accompaniment to the action. A complete score *could* be prepared: but we feel that a more stimulating result might be attained if the music were to be improvised during rehearsals, following the rhythm of the stage directions – it could be done with one instrument only. The stage directions might be read aloud with the music at early stages of rehearsal, to accompany the action: then the reading could be dropped and the music retained. We are aware that this sounds very vague and perhaps impracticable: but we had hoped to experiment in such a way with *Friday's Hiding*.

We did, however, succeed in obtaining the services of a group of students to perform some improvisations round the theme of this play while we were writing it. Their work materially affected the shape of the finished text. They were:

> Maurice Burgess
> Frank Challenger
> George Dorosh
> Delia Jones
> Mary Saunders
> Linda Watkins

– all of the School of Art, Shrewsbury. We are most grateful for their assistance, and also that of their drama director, Albert Hunt.

M.D'A. & J.A.

*Friday's Hiding* was first produced at the Royal Lyceum Theatre, Edinburgh, on 29 March 1966 with the following cast:

| | |
|---|---|
| JOHN BALFOUR, *a Farmer* | Callum Mill |
| MISS LETITIA BALFOUR, *His Sister* | Lennox Milne |
| EDDIE ⎱ *Labourers*<br>WILLIE TAM ⎰ | David Kincaid<br>Brian Cox |

Directed by Sheila Ronald and Tom Fleming

The scene is a Farm (both within doors and out) in the Lowlands of Scotland.

The time is the present.

MISS BALFOUR.

*There was an auld dour skinflint of a farmer*
*His name was John Balfour*
*He lived with nae wife but a weary auld sister*
   *Her name was Elspeth Letitia*
                  *That's me*
   *They call me Aunt Letty.*


*Forbye he was rich eneuch to marry a Laird's dochter*
*Forbye he was rich eneuch to pay his farm-hands better.*


   *Twa young men he had*
                  *That's Eddie and Willie Tam*
   *But they're young men nae langer*
   *They've dug and delved John Balfour's land*
   *Seventeen year wi' never a rise in wages*
   *And they're lucky to get what they do get*


*For every Friday*
            *That's pay-day*
*He gangs to the bank in the forenoon to draw out the money*
*But in the afternoon whaur is he? Whaur does he meet them to*
   *pay them?*


EDDIE.

*Dear goodness he meets us in nae place*
*But he hides awa, fast, like the wee man he is,*
*In the house or the barn or the yard or the field*
               *or under the bank of the burn or*
                           *awa yonder on the fell*
               *or onywhere else I canna think of nor tell*
*For Friday for Balfour is nocht but the day he's in hiding*
*And before we get paid we maun find him.*
*Has he been to the bank yet?*

WILLIE TAM.
*He hasna come back yet.*
*We maun wait in the yard and waylay him.*
*He'll be wanting his dinner within.*

Aunt Letty in the kitchen lays out John Balfour's dinner.

MISS BALFOUR.
*I want my money too.*
*I canna buy the man meat without it.*
*He willna even gie it to his ain sister, consider it!*

ALL THREE OF THEM. *Dear goodness, what a man!*

John Balfour, hame frae the bank, looks into the yard
he sees his two labourers on the watch, he retires.

 The pair of them, weary with waiting, bring out their bread
 and kebbuck, contrive to keep an eye on the gate, but grow
 careless.
John Balfour throws a stone, it goes over their heads,
hits the wall on yon side of them, they turn toward it – suspi-
cious –
then creep over there and watch, their backs turned towards
his entry.

 Which he makes, concealed in a haycock.

 The Haycock sneezes.

 They turn at the noise.
 There is nocht but a Haycock.
 Whaur the hell did that come from?
 They look at it – dubious –
a dog barks beyond the house, distracts their attention, they
swing around and run over there.

 The Haycock moves again.

 This time, when they turn back to continue their watching
 and waiting and eating

it is that degree nearer the porch of the house.
Willie Tam observes this but doesna care to tell Eddie
lest Eddie think him daft.
But unobtrusively he paces the distance between the Haycock
and the house and Eddie sees him do it.
　　Eddie does it himself.
　　By God it *is* nearer.
They are not at all sure they want to meddle with this.
　　if Mr Balfour should choose to walk home inside a Haycock
　　it is not for the likes of them to interfere with his fancy.
　　But none the less they want their money.

They retire to consider the possibilities of some action.
As they whisper together the Haycock moves
They see it move
　　　　　　　　　　and run forward
　　　　　　　　　　　　　　　　but too late
　　It is at the door.

　　Mr Balfour is in his ain kitchen
　　and the Haycock's whisked awa.

John Balfour, safe at last where they canna get after him
without breach of etiquette
transfers the weekly money
counts out certain banknotes – these into a cashbox
(lock it, put it away, lock the cupboard, carefully replace both
keys on the end of his watchchain into the watchchain pocket) –
these notes, till now retained under a careful stern thumb,
go in their turn, wrapped in an old fold of dry paper,
　　into his wallet.
　　a worn wallet, tight, fastened with farmer's twine, into the
　　inner breast pocket, button it up. Good.
Sit down to your dinner, mean old devil.
Poor Letty serves it up. She's had hers already. Sit sideways to
table, eat potatoes off your knife, heavy movements with your

eating irons, vulgar old devil, aye, ye *would* read the *Farmer's Weekly* propped up on the salt-cellar.

What's the matter with her? She's got her fingers on the edge of the table, tap-tapping there like a leaf against the window.

Rap her on the knuckles with the back edge of your knife. No, you'd better not, she is your ain sister.

What the de'il is she after?

MISS BALFOUR.
*Housekeeping money, John, Friday . . .?*

Bedamned to that. He's wanting his cup of tea.

Are ye no gaun to pour it out, woman? That's better. Aye, ye can drink a cup yersel. Set down to it and gie ower demonstrating your damned fidgets.

He lights up his pipe with a great deal of profound hesitation.

Willie Tam and Eddie at their dinners in the yard
are slow over bread and kebbuck,
dry it is, slow between the teeth.
Get up and gie the auld woman your can to be filled.
She takes it in at the back door and hands it back full of tea.
She gives them one or two significant looks.
She's telling them, ye ken, he has the money frae the bank,
But lockit up,
         lockit,
                 ye canna get it yet.
Ach, awa wi' that, they'll drink their tea and bide their time.

EDDIE.
*Seventeen year I've dug and delved his fields*
*He's offered me ne'er a raise in wages.*
*Nor you neither? Aye, aye, nor you neither:*
*Begod this very day I'm gaun to mak shift and ask him.*

WILLIE TAM.
*Ye'll never dae it.*

Aye aye but Eddie will, but he'll have to catch him first. Mean auld devil and they glare at his back door.

He's finished his tea and reconsidered the front page of the *Farmer's Weekly* (having read the whole paper from front to back first), reconsidered the middle page, thought seriously about something else upon the back page, folded it up, once, twice, and again, to about the size of a flatiron, then carefully places it on one end of the mantelpiece on top of last week's issue and sixteen weeks before that.

A great deal of profound hesitation once again with his pipe that has to be knocked out and drawn upon and generally supervised,

> Then a slow trudge to the door
> taking no notice of the auld sister,
> stand in the door, meeting the regard of the two labourers.

> They look wages at him, grind their teeth in wages,
> shuffle wages with their feet (to which they are risen)
> But he takes no damn notice.

> Only indicates the dungforks
> they are to work with this afternoon and away he goes from
> them.
> Minding his own business, minding it severely.
> His own business is a hoe. He selects it,
> And all upon his own with a hoe upon his shoulder he leaves
> them
> > alone in the yard.

> Once out of their sight he runs.
> Aunt Letty clears the table and clears herself off.
> She has a sad thought about the cash box
> lockit up and awa – eh deary me . . .

Dungforks up, dung on the dungforks,
swing it up, the pair of ye, slow swings but experienced

from the midden to the cart, loading it up.
This'll no get us our wages.
But it's little good to rush it. Fork a bit further.
Whaur the hell's he gone?
He took a hoe, he's in the Lang Field,
Eddie's awa to find him.

    Willie Tam's dubious,
    but Eddie's the boy,
               angry,
                       he wants his siller,
         he's awa.
Willie Tam stacks the forks, gangs after, not happy.

Into the Lang Field, where Balfour sets his cold eye
considering the furrows and the work of his hoe;
commences his slow bend, drives his weapon,
all upon his own and a mile from the house.
Finishing the first row, he looks up
                       and there they are.

    The pair of them glaring.
    Good God they want their money.

Up to the head of the second row, let them follow if they want
to.

    They want to.

Stoop again, hoe again, he's all upon his own,
neither word nor look given to acknowledge their existence.
The three of them together move, backwards, down the field.
End of the second row,
                  Good God they're still beside him.

So up the field again to the head of the third.
    A pair of daft bridesmaids grinning ingratiation.
    Ah well, John Balfour's no such a bad fellow at heart.

He cracks a wee smile in return, leans on his hoe,
hand to his pocket, slowly slowly slowly
does he mean to pay them already?
                he does not.
He has tobacco in his pocket
and a great deal of profound hesitation
toward replenishment of his pipe.

WILLIE TAM.
*It's a grand afternoon, Mr Balfour.*

EDDIE.
*It's Friday afternoon, Mr Balfour.*

Aye, so it is, it's a fine time of day for the enjoyment of a
pipe.
Then the hoe propped on its end in the furrow
is somehow transferred from John Balfour to poor Eddie,
who, mollified by the humanity of the farmer's rare smile
and the contentment expressed by the farmer's humane pipe,
cannot, as a Christian, do other than take the hoe
   and commence the third row.

At the end of each row Eddie smiles at the farmer
but fails to speak.
Backwards and forwards he works. John Balfour takes his ease.
Willie Tam is silly Willy, fidgeting and grinning.
He minds the dungfork labour has yet to be concluded,
bobs his apologies and trudges to conclude it.
   John Balfour looks after him,
                     considers,
                           calls him back,
they are all three of them to work at the hoeing, after all,
   so Willie Tam must trudge and fetch a pair of hoes.

Eddie finishes his third row, smiles and comes to his master,
smiles again, opens his mouth –

EDDIE.
*Friday . . .*

John Balfour didna hear him, he says it again,
He meets John Balfour's eye and pretends he hadna spoken.
   To them baith returns Willie Tam,
   one hoe for himself
                        and another for the master,

   Thus we have three men stooping
   Working together backwards,
   Two of them wondering when's he going to give them
   their money
   One of them wondering how the devil to avoid giving it,
   And he works in the middle.

So they swop glances, (that would be nudges, were they nearer)
across his bended back. Eddie gives vent
to certain dismal menaces, swinging up his hoe
and feigning to bring it down on the devoted head of Balfour,
thereby he terrifies the gentle soul of Willie Tam,
continuing as he does with a pantomime of cruel violence,
first: to hoe John Balfour's head – then: to jump upon his
body – then:
to stamp down upon his vitals and rifle his waistcoat pocket.
There is such exaggeration in the finale of this mime
that Willie Tam begins to laugh and John Balfour hears him
laugh,
looks rapidly up at him and then up at Eddie
who at that moment is executing his dance of triumph
to celebrate his rehearsed rapine
and is forthwith compelled by the cold eye of the master
to turn the dance into the pursuit with hoe and hand
of a non-existent wasp, which he murders
just in time to save John Balfour from a non-existent sting.

John Balfour is not grateful and shows that there are many
                                                furrows yet to hoe.
But Willie Tam is more amused by the discomfiture of Eddie
and laughs
and laughs
and laughs
                    across John Balfour's back.

Eddie thereupon rages within him,
and there are serious signs that he really will attack
Balfour
and if Willie Tam isna careful he'll catch a bang as well –
here's a hunk of a boulder that would pulverize John
                                                Balfour's brain pan
and here's a hob-nailed boot-toe for his quick emascula-
tion.

Eddie stops his work.

He is at the end of a row.
Balfour comes backward towards him,
when he reaches him, by God, there is about to be
a terrible conjunction of crisis – look at the hoe,
how it is gripped in Eddie's angry hand.
Look how he signals Willie Tam to stand by him and
look how Willie Tam in great fear would dissuade him –

    and backwards comes Balfour,
                            unaware,
                                    stooped,
                                            vulnerable.
He works right up to the boot of Eddie
                                    and he stops.
He doesna get up but contemplates the weed penultimately
dislodged
considering maybe that he would have done better to have
dislodged it deeper . . .

EDDIE.
*Friday. Mr Balfour, it's Friday.*

If he were to look up now he would see the two men
– there they stand – about to beat him and to shake their
money out of him.
But without lifting his body one hand's-breadth

>he runs away sideways
>dropping his hoe
>away over furrow and ditch
>out of the field-gate

before either Eddie or Willie Tam are even aware he has
gone.
How stupid they stand there.

EDDIE.
*Awa, man, let's get him!*

Seventeen years of suppressed oppressed hard labour
are running after Balfour and God kens what they'll dae to
him –
supposing they should catch him.

>For the first time ever

John Balfour is afraid of his men.
And yet for Godsake they would never be so violent
as to actually damage him –

>oho though would they not!

And he looks out from behind a thorn hedge and sees them
come running
across the clayey ridges, their hoes in their hands,
he dodges round the bush, he is quicker than they are,
they think they have him surrounded but he dodges round
again,
then he's off and out of sight and they stand and look stupid.

>Then after him again

and he seeks for bush after bush
using each one for cover until
he is flushed out of it,
dodging hither and thither
but never in a panic,
using his intelligence,
which, he is ever confident,
is more than twice as sharp as theirs.

Down into a ditch and he pulls a bush over him,
they leap the ditch without noticing
find nobody beyond it, cast in different directions around,
draw together again frustrated, and take counsel
at the very edge of the ditch where he lies.

Their fury is more than a bit abated.

Eddie pulls out tobacco and papers to roll himself a wee
smoke
               and one for Willie Tam.
Willie Tam strikes a match, the wind blows it out.
Willie Tam strikes another match, blown out in like manner.
He has but the one more match left to him in the box:
He strikes it,
          and endeavouring to conceal it from the wind
          succeeds with it in burning the tips of his fingers.
          Curses it
          Drops it.
          Through the leaves in the ditch
          On to Mr Balfour's face.
          Mr Balfour cries out
          (not very surprisingly)

And they see who it is and they pull the bush off him.
He slithers out unabashed
but he kens what to do.
Before they can assess their own attitude toward him

he has his own matchbox out and
   has offered them a light.

Gracious goodness but now they are under an obligation to the
man.

They must accordingly help him to his feet and dust him down
they must replace the odds and ends that are falling out of his
pockets
they must pretend with great embarrassment
that they meant no more than rough humour.
He's a crude carl himself, he will understand their notion of a
joke
and he appears to understand it for he laughs with them
                    accommodatingly.
                    But keeps his hand
                    (as it were by accident)
                    pressed hard on his wallet-pocket.

He minds their purposes yet, which they seem to have
forgotten.
But not for aye – they've remembered them now,
for here in Eddie's helpful fist is the loose dangle of John's
watchchain
with the cashbox keys upon it.

John Balfour sees he sees them,
he kens the clicketty-click in Eddie's slow brain –

EDDIE.
*Friday . . . Why, Friday, it is . . .*

And Balfour's awa again,
shot from his grasp and running like a weasel,
stuffing chain and keys within him as he runs,
and where does he run to?
This time clear of ploughland hedge and ditch
deep into the thickets – whinbush bramble blackthorn,

and the pair of them after him
struggling falling cursing.

> They have him
> and they've lost him.

Eddie gets a strong hold of him
but he drags himself clear and by force of his dragging
throws himself across to the nervous grab of Willie Tam
knocks Willie in the belly, rebounds clear towards Eddie
dodges Eddie, knocking Eddie with his foot under the
chin,
Eddie falls backward, Willie Tam's already fallen,
John Balfour's foot went too much upward,
he dances back upon one leg
he's no a stork, he's a man, he canna sustain it,
he's arsy-versy over in the matt of the blackthorn.

And the pair of them are up and jump in upon him terribly.

They grab him up, he slumps under,
they hoick his feet, his arms hang heavy,
they stoop and lift his head, they shake it and it lolls.

> Good God have they murdered him?
> It looks damn well like it.
>
> They are stricken men.

They are all in a fluster with penitence
and hang above John Balfour's body
slapping his cheeks and feeling his bone-joints
and attempting many contradictory forms of resuscitation.
Then with a look from one to the guilty other
they hoist him up betwixt them
and hump him home to his house.
His head hangs like a dead head
and their remorseful steps as they carry him
are as heavy as lead . . .

Aunt Letty in the kitchen, doing a bit of dusting,
Hears their slow tramp as it comes across the yard
and she looks through the window in a passing curiosity
sees what there it to see
            drops her duster in horror and flies out to meet them

assailing the cortège with weeping and wailing
and ungirdled reproaches and strikings at their heads.
She pulls John Balfour in more or less in spite of them
and has him sprawled upon a sofa
and hot water and cold water and poultices and compresses
and smelling-salts and iodine and all the other condiments
rushed in and applied in a fury of commiseration.

            But she's no sae simple, Aunt Letty.

    In a frenzy of grief she may be but she minds her proper
    interests
    and in all the whirlpool muddle of sickbed assiduities
    she cunningly unhooks her brother's keys
    from the end of his watchchain and
            slips them in her apron pocket.

Eddie and Willie Tam, distracted, fail to notice.
There is no sign of life from the prostrate master of the house.
And sorrowfully, inch by inch, his kinswoman and his depen-
dants
accept and recognize the inevitability of death.

    He was all that *she* had
    And who will employ *them* now?
    And a cloth is drawn across his face
    And they turn away in gloom.

MISS BALFOUR.
*I'll mak ye a cup o' tea.*

And she begins this necessary work of mercy and consolation
with heavy heart.

But the keys in her apron jingle-jingle some small reassurance.

Of course the man's not dead at all,
(this is a comedy)
and after a while he lifts back the cloth
peeps out, sits up. They're all at their tea.
Not one of them to bother to look around at him.
What in the de'il's name's been happening?
And who for Godsake put this cloth upon his face?
With a shrug he pulls out his pipe
and is about to strike a match and light it
when he recollects
                at last he recollects
that there had been some sort of nonsense about the men's
wages.
In his pocket is his wallet, he takes it out – quietly –
subtracts the folded paper with the banknotes within it
puts the wallet into the pocket – quietly –
and sets the money on the mantelpiece
            in two careful piles

          and nobody's noticed.

Then he strikes the match for his pipe.
Ho ho they notice now.

But being of a sombre northern race they do not respond
                        to miracles.
Eddie and Willie Tam do however respond to the fact
that they are sitting in the master's kitchen chairs
without the master's express invitation
and they get up in a hurry and flatten themselves against
the walls.

Aunt Letty, frozen and angry that her grief was so premature
thrusts a cup of tea at John Balfour and sits down again, her
back turned.

He takes the cup to the table and sits and drinks it, smoking.

Willie Tam is edging his way to the door when his eye lights
     on the mantelpiece
     and he sees what is to be seen there.
     He nudges Eddie.
     Eddie sees it too.
     They clear their throats.
     John Balfour takes no notice.
     Eddie takes the money –
He appreciates the convention that it should not
be acknowledged as being there at all, thereby
saving all and sundry from expressions of gratitude
for what is after all only due to them by right,
and he pockets his own pile and hands Willie Tam his.
They nod their heads and knuckle forelocks in a perfunc-
tory manner.
John Balfour takes no notice.
Aunt Letty takes no notice
        her back to all three of them.
So the two men work themselves bashfully towards the door.

At last *they have been paid* and one more Friday's toils are over.
     Or are they?
     Willie Tam thinks so.
     But Eddie recollects.
     He stops short in the doorway,
     obstructing Willie Tam.
     He clears his throat.

EDDIE.
*A rise . . .*

WILLIE TAM (*restrainingly*).
*Na na . . .*

EDDIE.
*Ah, ah, a rise in wages – seventeen year . . .*

Eddie is gey determined and courage fills up his demeanour.
He strides across the room to Mr Balfour's foursquare back
And claps him hard upon it.

EDDIE.
*A rise, a rise, Mr Balfour, I mean to ask ye for a rise.*

John Balfour heard him the first time and has sat struck rigid
with pipe and tea-cup
now he spills his tea and drops his pipe in the puddle.
Aunt Letty too, half-risen, can scarce believe her ears,
while Willie Tam would like to creep under the teapot.
    John Balfour turns and stares.
    This is beyond his comprehension.
    Slowly he rises up.
    He paces the room, so slowly,
    back and forth in amazement
    three times altogether paces the room,
        then he stops.
        He puts his face before the quailing face of Eddie
        till the noses are all but touching.

BALFOUR.
*What for !*

    Eddie can think of no answer.
    Aunt Letty thinks of it for him.

MISS BALFOUR.
*John, the cost of living. He's a man with a family . . .*

    John Balfour, in furious contempt at this,
        dances and spins,
        laughs, whirls his arms,
        seizes the *Farmer's Weekly*
        and dashes it on the ground.

Eddie, the miserable coward, implicates a poor neutral.

EDDIE.
*Willie Tam wants a rise too.*

> Willie Tam is now spun upon by the dervish John
> Balfour,
> he retreats in bewildered terror,
> then, gripped on the elbow by Eddie,
> remembers he's a man and stands up for his rights.

WILLIE TAM.
*Aye aye aye – we baith want a rise . . .*

> John Balfour flings him from him and spins and whirls
>> saucers
>> his coat tails fly, his watchchain leaves its moorings
>> Then he stops.
>> Then he crouches.
>> Then he advances upon Willie Tam,
>> thrusting up at him a trembling finger,
>> his knees are bent double beneath him
>> his eye is like a pitchfork point.

BALFOUR.
*You! Why, you're a single man!*

Then he throws himself upon the table, sits there cross-legged
and cackles with rage, dominating the whole kitchen.
Old gnome, he reassembles the dishevelled ends of his accoutrements
including
> his watchchain
>> which he finds
>>> has no keys on it.
>>> Where are the keys?
>>> Aunt Letty has the keys.

>> And furthermore she has, for the first time,
>> her own appropriate rage.

She throws herself utterly upon these sordid men

and brandishing the keys and brandishing a toasting fork
she clears them all from the kitchen
tumbling one over the other head over heels to avoid her
                                        out into the yard.
  When the door is fast bolted, she is left alone within.
  So she opens the cupboard and then opens the cash box.
  She takes out all the money – and there is a fair quantity
too –
  she sits down at the table and enjoys her *coup d'état*.

  Also in the cupboard is John Balfour's personal whisky.
  She fills up a tea-cup and she sits and she drinks.
  She picks up the *Farmer's Weekly* and the other cups and
so forth
  and clears them all away.
    Then somehow she's no sae blithe.
    She's got one cup and saucer before her
    and heretofore there has always been at least one other.
    She sets a second one out again and looks at it . . .
  Then she bethinks her of something that was said.
  Then she bethinks her of an auld kist that lies behind the
door.
  She pulls it out and opens it.
                    She takes out of it
                    (wrapped and camphored)
                    what must have been
                    her mother's original wedding dress
                    long kept in vain for herself.

It's a large full-skirted Edwardian garment,
far too large for her dried-up wee body
and it goes on very easily on top of her ordinary clothes.
She holds it up against her,
                    and then she puts it on.
                    Then she sits down again
                    and broods on possibilities.

John Balfour is the first of the three to attempt to get in
again.
He forces the catch of the window with a bent bit of wire
and with a great deal of difficulty puts his head through it.
Two moonlike faces in the aperture behind him
are Eddie and Willie Tam,

                  who goggle at the wedding dress.


John Balfour considers the pros and the cons.
Suppose she were to marry Willie Tam?
To pay for the pair of them would no doubt come even
cheaper
than to pay them both separately as he has to do now.
He calculates this on his fingers out there in the yard.
Then, very carefully, he scrambles

                through
                        the window.
He tiptoes to his sister and clears his throat, carefully,
She doesna turn upon him, so he emboldens himself.


And he opens the door and beckons in Eddie and Willie Tam.
Willie Tam bethinks him of something that was said
And he willna come in so Mr Balfour has to pull him.
Once he's in, John Balfour makes an effort to improve his
appearance,
Sprucing him up, quickly, and thrusting a cauliflower
in at his button-hole to give the semblance of a bridegroom
then, playing the Best Man, he leads him grandly up
to majestic Aunt Letty
and presents him, with deference.

    She accepts him.
    She embraces him.
    Willie Tam can make no protest,
    so large and preposterous is her embracement.
    And she gives John Balfour back his keys.

Then John Balfour pours out whisky
   into everybody's cup
   with leaping generosity,
   back-smacking, laughing hugely,
   the whole bottle is lavishly emptied,
   he grabs another bottle from the inside of the cupboard
   and he pours that out as well.

He kisses his sister's cheeks and he slaps her on the hurdies
and he sits them all down and indicates Liberty Hall.
He himself, the gracious host, the indulgent brother-in-law
presides as is fitting, patriarchally, in the middle.

   Yet at the same time, unobtrusively,
   he puts all the money back
   into the cash box, locks it up,
   and he puts the cash box back
   into the cupboard, locks it up,
   and he puts the keys back
   on to his watchchain and he puts that back
                          into his waistcoat pocket.

Then he resumes his ease amongst the party,
where Eddie is highly delighted and Willie Tam is making the
best of it
and only Aunt Letty is beginning to wonder how much longer
this foolishness will go on. She mops up spilled whisky.
   John Balfour raises his voice in song.
   The tune was once the tune of a metrical psalm
   but the words are his own and the men join in the refrains.
   If they thought about it twice they would not, but this is a
   party.

BALFOUR.
*The devil sure had done his work*
*And put us all in misery*
*But now concordance is restored*
*And here we sit and we agree.*

CHORUS.

*And we agree and we agree*
*And we agree in harmony.*

BALFOUR.

*What was a while turned up-side-down*
*Is now once more turned right-side-up*
*The master has his blessing gien*
*And poured y'all out a cheerful cup.*

CHORUS.

*And poured us out and poured us out*
*The auld white ewe has a strong black tup.*

BALFOUR.

*Then let us drink and never think*
*We can ourselves improve our life*
*Unless the master take the lead*
*We shall find nocht but grief and strife.*

CHORUS.

*We shall find nocht we shall find nocht*
*Till every man controls his wife*
*Till every fork lies under the knife*
*Till every plate kens its place in the larder*
*And every slate sticks to the rafter*
*And one gangs first and the rest gang after*
*That's what we call restoring order.*

The last refrain, being longer than the others, takes on the quality of a round song. And they sing it and sing it until the whisky restores its own sort of order and God kens how much work will be done in the fields this Saturday . . . Aunt Letty kens all right. She takes off the wedding dress and folds it up as neat as ever it was and lays it back in the kist and puts the kist back behind the door and sits down again in patience, mopping up spilled whisky and watching that the cups do not get broken.

# Methuen's Modern Plays

EDITED BY JOHN CULLEN

| John Mortimer | *Lunch Hour and other plays* |
| | *Two Stars for Comfort* |
| Joe Orton | *Loot* |
| Harold Pinter | *A Slight Ache and other plays* |
| | *The Birthday Party* |
| | *The Room and The Dumb Waiter* |
| | *The Caretaker* |
| | *The Collection and The Lover* |
| | *The Homecoming* |
| | *Tea Party and other plays* |
| Jean-Paul Sartre | *Crime Passionnel* |
| Theatre Workshop and Charles Chilton | *Oh What a Lovely War* |

★　　★　　★

# *Methuen's Theatre Classics*

| THE TROJAN WOMEN | Euripides |
| | *an English version by Neil Curry* |
| THE REDEMPTION | *adapted by Gordon Honeycombe from five cycles of Mystery Plays* |
| IRONHAND | Goethe |
| | *adapted by John Arden* |
| THE WILD DUCK | Ibsen |
| BRAND | *translated by Michael Meyer* |
| THE MASTER BUILDER | |
| HEDDA GABLER | |
| LADY WINDERMERE'S FAN | Wilde |
| THE IMPORTANCE OF BEING EARNEST | |
| THE PLAYBOY OF THE WESTERN WORLD | Synge |

✱　　✱　　✱